INVESTING WITH GIANTS

Tried and True Stocks That Have Sustained the Test of Time

INVESTING WITH GIANTS

TRIED AND TRUE STOCKS THAT HAVE SUSTAINED THE TEST OF TIME

Linda T. Mead

John Wiley & Sons, Inc.

Published by John Wiley & Sons, Inc., New York.
Published simultaneously in Canada.

This publication is designed to provide accurate and authoritative information in
regard to the subject matter covered. It is sold with the understanding that the
publisher is not engaged in rendering professional services. If professional advice
or other expert assistance is required, the services of a competent professional
person should be sought.

ISBN 0-471-41337-2

Printed in the United States of America.

10 9 8 7 6 5 4 3 2 1

Dad and Essie

Contents

APPENDIX I   Investing Resources   141

APPENDIX II   Annual Reports—Letters to Shareholders
                   through the Decades *with Procter & Gamble
                   and Johnson & Johnson*   145

                   Glossary of Investing Terms   225

                   Index   249

Foreword

As American as mom and apple pie? How about as American as Chevrolet, Coca-Cola, and McDonald's? While those products are immediately associated with the United States, in reality, they are part of the global economy and the companies that produce them are truly giants in our world. They were not always giants. Most had humble beginnings and grew in different ways.

McDonald's has come a long way since Ray Kroc decided to get into the business of serving hamburgers and fries by buying out the McDonald brothers and opening his two restaurants in 1955. No longer do the signs outside of the restaurants indicate the number of hamburgers served as they once did. Instead they merely state, "billions and billions." Not only are the Golden Arches a welcome sight to Americans traveling abroad, but people from all over the world have accepted fast food as part of their diet. When the company first opened in Moscow, well before the Iron Curtain was parted, Russians lined up for blocks to partake in that most American of meals. Through it all, McDonald's has remained a fast food company. While there have been modifications to the menu, the company has stuck with what it knows best.

Other giants have taken a different path. Philip Morris, for example, began to acquire other companies and operations, such as Miller Brewing, Seven-Up, and General Foods. They acquired their own paper company and opened bottling plants. General Motors was not always GM. It began as Olds Motor and William Durant began what we know today by combining Buick and Oldsmobile. It then added Cadillac and Pontiac, both independent operations before Durant added them to what would become the largest automobile manufacturer in the world.

Tracing the history and looking at business decisions of these and other household names makes for a fascinating study. How did IBM go from being referred to as the "Itty Bitty Machine Company" to "Big Blue"? When asked what the market was for Coke products, the chairman once said, "The four billion people who wake up thirsty every morning." Johnson & Johnson management recognized that there had to be a lot more scraped knees if its Band-Aid brand were to continue to grow. Through research and development, along with some strategic acquisitions, Johnson & Johnson diversified its products and took advantage of its vast distribution system.

Learning how to find out about developments through common sense and study is revealed in *Investing with Giants: Tried and True Stocks That Have Sustained the Test of Time*, by Linda Mead, and guides the individual through the process. In this age of rapid information, investors many times misinterpret announcements, basing investment decisions on stock prices instead of looking at the long-term potential. Reading and analyzing an annual or interim report can be revealing. It offers an individual investor an opportunity to weigh what can happen to a company in years to come. Statistics I have seen indicate that a shareowner of a company spends 15 to 25 minutes looking at an annual report of a company. That's less time than the same person spends balancing a checkbook, even though an investment in a company can have much more significance financially. Linda makes reading a financial report a learning process. Whether you are simply considering investing in a new company, or own a large block of stock, you will benefit from her experience and observations.

Ken Janke

President and CEO
National Association of
Investors Corporation

Acknowledgments

No more than a handful of authors can say that they alone wrote their books. I am not one of them so I will acknowledge those who have helped make this book a reality.

Agent Nancy Ellis for running with an idea and keeping me on track.

Editor Deborah Englander, for supporting ideas that come her way, along with the Wiley staff for their expertise.

Howard Fisher for believing and just being there.

Andrea Brown for her very bendable ear.

Susie Farber for helping me to find the light at the end of the tunnel.

Laurel Newby and Janetta Roach for their invaluable assistance and research.

Mom for understanding my propensity for procrastination.

My partners at LitWest Group for helping me juggle.

Anyone who asked "how's it going?"

Also, I am most grateful to:

Sue Peterman and Kenneth Janke of the NAIC

Stephen Sanborn of Value Line Investment Survey

Elisabeth King of Johnson & Johnson

Lisa Morrelli and Edward Rider of Procter & Gamble

Ira Galtman of American Express

Coca-Cola Archives

Gary Burke of NASDAQ

Introduction

Prior to the second half of the 20th century, investing in the stock market had been almost exclusively an activity of the wealthy. Wall Street brokerages were at the disposal of the moneyed few. But, in recent years, the plethora of information that has become available to the masses through magazines, organizations, TV, radio and, ultimately, the Internet, have given a new face to investing—both yours and mine.

Investing in the stock market doesn't have to be a deep, dark mystery. Today, we have available educational resources based on the premise that investing is a matter of common sense. In his article from the January 2001 issue of *Better Investing* magazine, Kenneth Janke, Sr., President and CEO of the National Association of Investors Corporation's Board of Trustees, explains what common sense means.

> Investing really is common sense. It begins with the three basic investment principles adopted by NAIC that are as much keys to investment success today as they were in 1951. Investing regularly and reinvesting earnings can be pretty much automatic. Some people have problems buying stocks in those companies that will do better than the market in general. Still, it isn't that hard to do, with just a little training and practice—something you're sure to get if you hang around the NAIC community for a while!
>
> Let's pretend you pick five stocks and invest $10,000 in each. There have to be some assumptions made in those selections. First, history tells us that the economy and companies in general can grow at around 4 percent annually over the long term and that the inflation rate will average about 3 percent. That's a compound rate of around 7 percent. It is reasonable for us to expect that our average selections should be able to increase earnings by that amount over time.

In your five picks, three of them are likely to end up only being average. Since stock prices reflect earnings progress over the long term, let's assume that those stocks will average 7 percent in price appreciation, a figure we try to exceed, but we all make mistakes. Let's assume one of the selections is a complete disaster and becomes worthless. Finally, let's assume the last one continues to grow at 15 percent, just as you predicted on your Stock Selection Guide study. Thus, only one of the five performs as expected. Not a very good batting average, but look how the portfolio would have performed (see Table I.1).

TABLE I.1   Portfolio Growth

	Five Years	*Ten Years*
Stock A	$ 0	$ 0
Stock B	14,026	19,672
Stock C	14,026	19,672
Stock D	14,026	19,672
Stock E	20,114	40,456
TOTAL	$62,192	$99,472

If the same $50,000 had been placed in a 5% Certificate of Deposit, the value at the end of five years would have grown to $63,814 and in 10 years it would have been $81,445. Even with average performance, the stocks would have done better over the ten-year period.

Investing is not brain surgery. You don't have to be right 99.9 percent of the time to build your wealth over the long term.[1]

Common sense investing also means knowing how to be prepared: become educated about companies, the stock market, and the economy. Every day the financial news networks and the Internet report on these matters. Potential investors can hear or read reports on the economic indicators that we discuss in Chapter Six, the movements of the various market indexes (Chapter Two), what specific

---

stocks or business sectors are doing, or go onto the Internet and look up stock prices and information about specific companies. Many people I know, including myself, have also formed investment clubs and joined the NAIC for educational purposes. In particular, the NAIC offers step-by-step beginner, intermediate, and advance classes in stock research, helpful software, books and magazines. These are only some of the resources available today to help you begin your investment future. And while we cannot absolutely predict the future of individual companies and the market as a whole, investing is certainly not akin to gambling when you do your homework. It is our intent to help you in this journey as we cover some of the following points in the book.

Invest in what you know

- Get a good historical perspective on any company you are considering investing in. Get to know the company intimately. All companies have websites with histories and complete product information as well as recent annual reports.

- Read the most recent annual reports cover to cover. You'll see how a company presents itself in light of what may be appearing in the news concerning that company. For example, how do they discuss recalls, lawsuits, earnings results?

- Learn how to evaluate a company's financial information from its annual report. The numbers don't lie. Understanding where a company stood financially in the past and where they might be going in the future can help in making a better judgment.

- Keep up with a company's news. TV coverage on financial news networks and Internet coverage on companies runs all day long. Know what will affect the company's future financial position.

Learn the art of buying stocks

- Buy for the long term. Individuals who buy one day and sell the next generally lose money. They are gamblers, not investors.

- Comparison shop. Learn as much about the competition's stock as the stock you are considering.

- Balance your portfolio. Learn how to mix large cap, medium cap, and small cap stocks for best results.

- Invest only in as many stocks as you feel you (or your investment club) can track on a quarterly basis. You can always build from there.

Although we are addressing only a few of the large cap "giants" in this book, we want to encourage readers to look at all stocks before assembling a portfolio. While many of the medium and small cap stocks will grow more quickly than large cap stocks and help raise the percentage return of your portfolio, it is the large cap stocks, the "blue chip" giants, that will tend to keep a portfolio grounded because they have less of a swing factor in a changing economy. Of course there are exceptions to every rule.

The purpose of this book is not to endorse any particular company, but to help in the educational process. We have selected some of the "tried and true" blue chip stocks presented in this book to give the investor an historical perspective on companies in various industries and how they have fared during the last 100 years.

The book is divided into two parts. In Part I, we begin with some basic history of the stock market, present information about market indexes and economic indicators that you hear about on a daily basis, and provide a step-by-step breakdown of the annual report and how to interpret the information it contains.

Part II of the book provides an historical time sequence governed by events or significant movements in our economy over the last 100 years. Each of these decades or eras had some affect on these giants of industry—some good and some bad. Understanding that companies cannot take their success for granted, the purpose is to discover how they continue to reinvent themselves to maintain growth through sales and earnings and stay successful. And with success comes investors. Everyone wants to invest in a winner, so the giants must be profitable and financially strong, about which information can be gathered from the annual report; deftly managed, as we learn from a company's history and annual reports; and competitive in the marketplace, which can be determined by surveying and knowing the competition.

As part of the time sequence, we have provided a somewhat different perspective of the CEO's "Letter to Shareholders" from the Annual Reports of Procter & Gamble and Johnson & Johnson in Appendix II. From the 1940s through the turn of the century, you can see how the "letter" was utilized over the decades as well as the kind of information provided. Notice how the CEOs address product development, growth, and change in each of the letters selected to be the most interesting in each decade.

One final word: education is key, but you'll also need to remember to be patient while learning. In time, we can all become successful investors.

PART ONE

INVESTING PRELIMINARIES

The Stock Market— Birth of a Concept

KEY TERMS

- commodity
  A good or service exchanged in the economic marketplace.

- exchange or stock exchange
  A marketplace where securities (goods or services) are bought and sold.

- IPO (initial public offering)
  The date that a security begins trading publicly on the stock market.

- Nasdaq (National Association of Securities Dealers Automated Quotation System)
  A computerized network for OTC trading; one of the three major stock exchanges in the U.S.

- New York Stock Exchange (NYSE)
  The oldest of the stock exchanges in the United States.

- over-the-counter trading (OTC)
  Trading facilitated by "Market Makers" who buy and sell individual securities not included on one of the exchanges or listed markets.

- Securities and Exchange Commission (SEC)
  The federal agency created to administer securities laws and protect the investing public.

WHAT IS THE STOCK MARKET? Simply put, it is a one-stop shopping place where you can purchase ownership in a company. This is by no means a new concept; it predates the birth of America by some 250 years. As far back as the 16th century, wealthy European merchants were investing in companies to make money, thus boosting their stature and rank of privilege. The place where men gathered to buy and sell these goods and services came to be known as an exchange. Their sales tallies were notched into a tree stump or a "stock" (giving rise to the term *to take stock*).

The birth of the stock market as a formal investing concept took place in 1553 when Sir Richard Willoughby, an English explorer, wanted to find a passage to the East. He formed the Muscovy Company to venture to Moscow. This first investment adventure, the very first IPO you might say, successfully returned loaded with exotic riches, thus lining the investors' pockets with gold. Satisfied investors helped launch the "stock market."

THE EXCHANGE

The first exchange, or stock exchange, as a place where traders gathered to speculate on merchandise, predated the Muscovy Company by some twenty years (1531) in the port city of Antwerp, Belgium. Following in Belgium's footsteps, exchanges were established in Hamburg, Germany, in 1558; Amsterdam, Holland, in 1619; and London and Paris toward the end of the 17th century—all of them wealthy and powerful centers for business and trade.

These earliest stock markets allowed for trade not only in actual products, but also in the possibility of future harvests and shiploads of commodities. But speculation of this sort was accompanied by hard-learned lessons even then. A good example of this occurred in the 1600s when tulips became a worldwide craze and tulip bulbs became a much-sought-after commodity. Not only were the bulbs bought and sold on exchanges, people began buying a share or portion of a single bulb. When the fad waned in 1637, investors pulled their money out en masse, triggering a market crash. In spite of England's South Sea Company speculation loss of some 37 million pounds in 1720, there existed an endless list of joint-stock companies, appropriately called "bubbles."

With the expansion and growth of each country, nations soon began to trade beyond their borders in search of more goods. The need for capital grew proportionately, resulting in "trading companies." The first widely-held and best known was the historic Dutch East India Company of Holland, set up in 1599.

The first U.S. exchanges opened in 1790 in Philadelphia, then the nation's financial center. Two years later, 20 brokers started the New York Stock Exchange (NYSE)—a far cry from today's 1,420 members. The New York Stock Exchange, though created in 1792, would not become the powerhouse of the nation's commercial life until 1817 when funding was needed to build the Erie Canal. With 19th century industrialization, the face of the stock market was forever changed. The need for capital to expand industries and shipping increased at break-neck speed. This stimulated the growth of new technologies, which we see even to this day. In 1846, the advent of the telegraph, which allowed the rapid transmission of information, fueled the stock market's growth with the first NYSE ticker-quote stock price in 1867.

SINCE NEW YORK housed the trading ports, Philadelphia had to wait for the arrival of coaches that carried information and traders from New York's port to Philadelphia in order to get shipping news. Not too long after, signal stations perched on New Jersey hilltops replaced coaches. A signalman with a telescope received codes flashed by light and immediately turned around to transmit the information by light to the next hilltop. News moved from New York to Philadelphia in only 10 minutes. This seemingly primitive system remained in place until the advent of the telegraph in 1846.

It wasn't until the Crash of 1929 that the next important advance occurred. The Crash of 1929 (lasting through 1932) prompted the creation of the Securities and Exchange Commission (SEC) in 1934 to oversee the market, mandating company accountability and responsibility to investors. With renewed faith in the stock market, investor numbers grew from 2 million in 1940 to 25 million in 1970.

Now, more expansive than ever, there are more than 33 million individual shareholders in the U.S. market. Including holders of both shares and mutual funds, the number of U.S. market investors is 48.5 million. Additionally, if we include retirement savings accounts and pension plans, the investor total climbs to over 84 million in the U.S. market alone.

HOW TECHNOLOGY CHANGED THE MARKET

With the technological advances offered by the Internet's interactive capabilities, together with the volume and speed of processing and exchanging information, we have seen the stock market burgeon by reaching out directly to investors. Today, one does not require a broker to receive information about a company or to make a trade. This of course raises other issues that we examine in this book: information gathering and guidance to help make wise investment decisions.

Technology and computerization have also brought about a revolution known as over-the-counter trading (OTC). Differing from the historic auction-style exchanges where traders gathered to buy and sell for investors, over-the-counter trading handles securities not listed on one of the exchanges or listed markets. Instead of traders, there are Market Makers[1] who buy and sell individual securities. The best known among these is the NASDAQ (National Association of Securities Dealers Automated Quotation System).

Established in 1971, this computerized network provides the best buying and selling prices of some 5,100 securities. There is no trading floor as with traditional exchanges, allowing for faster, free competition by independent dealers around the world. Interestingly, the computer technology that created the Nasdaq system also made the Nasdaq the largest stock market in dollar volume in the United

---

[1]Market Makers are securities firms that use their own capital to buy and maintain an inventory in a specific company's stock. When a Market Maker receives an investor's order to buy shares in a particular stock, it sells those shares to a customer from its existing inventory. If necessary, it will buy enough shares from another Market Maker to complete the sale.

States in 1999. Originally known to house small, growing companies with lesser capitalization than companies on the listed exchanges (where certain requirements must be met in terms of outstanding shares, market value, earnings, net tangibles assets and share price), many who now qualify for the NYSE have chosen to remain on the Nasdaq with their sister tech stocks.

> **B**OTH THE NASDAQ and the NYSE require that stocks maintain a trading price of at least $1. If a company trades for less than $1 per share for 30 consecutive trading days, the process of deleting begins.

Various other cities house their own stock exchanges and major worldwide exchanges number in the hundreds. Some of the most active include:

U.S. Exchanges

The Arizona Stock Exchange

Chicago Board of Options Exchange

Chicago Board of Trade

Chicago Mercantile Exchange

Chicago Stock Exchange

Kansas City Board of Trade

Minneapolis Grain Exchange

Pacific Stock Exchange

Philadelphia Stock Exchange

Other exchanges are housed in Canada, Mexico, South America, Africa, Europe, Scandinavia, Russia, the Middle East, Australia and New Zealand, and all of Asia, and the list keeps growing with the popularity of investing.

CHAPTER TWO

The Indexes

KEY TERMS

- average
  A weighted or unweighted evaluation of a market index.
- Dow Jones Industrial Average (DJIA)
  One of the most frequently quoted market indexes; a price-weighted average of 30 widely traded stocks.
- index
  A representative sampling of stocks, used to measure a particular industry or overall market movement.
- NASDAQ-100 Index
  A more recent market index concentrating on technological and new economy stocks.

To better understand the nature of the entire stock market and not rely on the change in any one stock, averages were developed, called market *indexes*. Today, we have a number of market indexes that reflect different aspects of the stock market: Dow Jones Industrial Average (DJIA), Standard & Poor's 500 (S&P 500), New York Stock Exchange Composite, NASDAQ-100, and a host of others.

The first and oldest among these indexes is the Dow Jones [Railroad] Average. In 1882, Charles H. Dow, Edward T. Jones, and Charles Bergstresser gathered and provided news and stock market observations daily in their "Customers' Afternoon Letter." To get a better beat on the market's ups and downs, which they reported to the public, Charles Dow devised an "average." It wasn't dubbed the DJIA until twelve years after the first "average" was posted. Charles Dow selected those stocks he thought were most representative of the general market at that time and posted the very first market average on July 3, 1884. This "industrial" average consisted of nine railroad stocks and two industrial stocks. They were:

> Chicago & Northwestern
>
> Delaware, Lackawanna & Western
>
> Lake Shore
>
> Louisville & Nashville
>
> Missouri Pacific
>
> New York Central
>
> Northern Pacific preferred
>
> Pacific Mail Steamship
>
> St. Paul
>
> Union Pacific
>
> Western Union

The average value of those eleven stocks was $69.93.

Contrary to how the DJIA index is computed today by using a set divisor, Dow's method of simple averaging—adding up the value of each stock and dividing by 11, the number of stocks at that time—gave each stock equal value or *weight*. Stocks were added and deleted by Dow, Bergstresser, and Jones over the next few years until, on July 8, 1889, the first issue of *The Wall Street Journal* (given its name by Bergstresser) was published and included a list of 39 traded stocks. This issue reported their opening, high, low, and closing prices. By 1896 there were two averages: the DJ Railroad Average, comprised of 20 railroad stocks; and the DJIA, comprised of 12 stocks in other industries. These original DJIA stocks were:

> American Cotton Oil
>
> American Sugar
>
> American Tobacco
>
> Chicago Gas
>
> Distilling & Cattle Feeding

General Electric

Laclede Gas

National Lead

North American

Tennessee Coal & Iron

U.S. Leather preferred

U.S. Rubber

THE AVERAGE PRICE of industrial stocks on May 26, 1896 was $40.94.

Formally named after the journalist with an idea, this average would become the pulse of stock activity in America.

By 1916, the DJIA had risen to a 20-stock average, and by 1928 the 30-stock average made its debut. Though remaining at a consistent 30 blue-chip U.S. stocks to this day, the average has altered its face with the changing times, with 15 adjustments between 1928 and 1986. It has shifted with the times as the economy changed from one based on agriculture to one based on industry and then on technology and information. General Electric is the only original stock still on the DJIA.

Today, the thirty stocks of the DJIA represent a cross section of all U.S. industries (see third column on Table 2.1) excluding transportation and utilities, which have their own averages. The movement of the average is measured in "points" rather than dollars. On a day-to-day basis, we hear that the average has moved up or down a certain number of points. This reflects the day's market in terms of these thirty stocks, and in general of all the other stock prices. The DJIA is not an indicator of the future, as many would have you believe. The economy and its many waverings are what can change the performance of individual stocks and the direction of the Dow. Evaluating movement can help us as individual investors by allowing us to view the past movement picture. Daily fluctuations are generally of no consequence, but the overall, long-term consequences of the market can be gleaned when we get a quarter-by-quarter picture of the market's movement,

TABLE 2.1 Dow Jones Industrial Average, February 9, 2001

Company Name	Ticker Symbol	Industry	Price	Weighting %
Alcoa Inc.	AA	Mining-non ferrous	37.099998	2.238
American Express Co.	AXP	Financial Services	47.029999	2.838
AT&T Corp.	T	Telecommunication	22.1000	1.333
Boeing Co.	BA	Aerospace	57.3400	3.460
Caterpillar Inc.	CAT	Machinery-Construction	43.0000	2.594
Citigroup Inc.	C	Financial Services	54.049999	3.261
Coca-Cola Co.	KO	Beverages-soft	60.139999	3.629
DuPont Co.	DD	Chemical	41.990002	2.534
Eastman Kodak	EK	Photo Equipment	44.790001	2.703
Exxon Mobil Corp.	XOM	Oil International	85.860001	5.181
General Electric Co.	GE	Diversified	45.6600	2.755
General Motors Corp.	GM	Auto	54.450001	3.285
Hewlett Packard Co.	HWP	Computer-mini	33.5000	2.021
Home Depot Inc.	HD	Building/Construction Retail	44.4300	2.681

Honeywell International Inc.	HON	Industry: Conglomerates	47.200001	2.848
IBM Corp.	IBM	Computer- mainframe	112.3200	6.778
Intel Corp.	INTC	Electrical Components-Semiconductor	33.5000	2.021
International Paper Co.	IP	Paper/Forest Products	36.599998	2.208
Johnson & Johnson	JNJ	Medical Supplies	94.980003	5.731
J.P. Morgan Chase & Co.	JPM	Bank	51.950001	3.135
McDonald's Corp.	MCD	Retail Restaurant	29.7600	1.795
Merck & Co.	MRK	Drugs	82.720001	4.992
Microsoft Corp.	MSFT	Computer Software	59.1250	3.568
Minnesota Mining & Manufacturing Co.	MMM	Diversified	110.66000	6.678
Philip Morris Cos.	MO	Tobacco	48.0000	2.896
Procter & Gamble Co.	PG	Household Products (soap/cleaning)	74.989998	4.525
SBC Communications Inc.	SBC	Utilities-Telephone	46.5700	2.810
United Technologies Corp.	UTX	Diversified	74.879997	4.518
Wal-Mart Stores Inc.	WMT	Retail-Discount	50.400002	3.041
Walt Disney Co.	DIS	Media Conglomerates	31.950001	1.928

which helps us project the market's future, whether "bull" or "bear" (see Chapter 3). The current roster of 30 stocks has not been changed since 1999 when Home Depot, Intel, Microsoft, and SBC Communications were introduced and Union Carbide, Goodyear Tire & Rubber, Sears, and Chevron were dropped.

Today the DJIA is not as simple a calculation as Charles Dow's original formula (total prices of stocks divided by number of stocks). The Dow is still referred to as an *unweighted* average, meaning that each company is valued by stock price and not company size. Hence, the greater the stock price, the greater its influence on the calculation of the average. The use of a specifically set divisor rather than the simple calculation began in 1992 when the average had to be adjusted for a two-for-one stock split by Coca-Cola in order to maintain the average and not create a distortion.

> IN TABLE 2.1, column 5 shows the *weighted* value of each of the Dow stocks on Friday, February 9, 2001. These weighting percentages change daily.

Here's the example of how a split would distort the average as explained by Dow Jones: If three stocks sell at $5, $10, and $15, their average price would be $10 ($5 + $10 + $15 = $30 ÷ 3 = $10). Let's say the $15 stock has a three-for-one stock split making the new price for that stock $5. The average now would be $6.67 ($5 + $10 + $5 (new price for the stock) = $20 ÷ 3 = $6.67). So to maintain the $10 average, an adjustment must be made to the stock that has just split. The divisor used by Dow Jones changes from time to time due to one of several occurrences: stock-splits, spin-offs, or component changes to the DJIA. This divisor is then divided into the day's total closing prices. And the resulting number shows us whether there is an increase or decrease in the DJIA compared with that of the previous day.

Check it out for a few days to see for yourself. Log on to *http://indexes.dowjones.com/djia_cos.html*.

You can do the same for the Dow Jones Transportation Average (DJTA), originally called the Railroad Average, and the Dow Jones Utility Average (DJUA), which was created in 1929.

If the DJIA drops dramatically in one day due to a particular stock (remember IBM's dramatic drop to 10 [adjusted for splits] in 1993?), you can calculate the impact of that individual stock on the overall index in this way: divide the stock's price change (difference between opening price and closing price) by the divisor at the time to see how many points that stock contributed to the change in the index on any given day. For instance, IBM stock fell $2.62 a share on May 30, 2001. Dividing that by the current divisor (.15369402) shows that IBM accounted for 17.04 of the Dow's 166.50-point decrease, or just over 10%.

THE DJIA INDEX DIVISOR is recalculated or adjusted for occurrences such as stock splits and spin-offs so that the stock's "weight" in the average remains consistent. Because of these adjustments made from time to time, the DJIA is not technically an average anymore, but is considered an indicator.

HOW STOCKS ARE SELECTED FOR THE DJIA

Today DJIA stocks are selected and maintained by the editors of *The Wall Street Journal* (published by Dow Jones & Co., Inc.) using these basic criteria:

1. The company must have a history of successful growth (worth the most in its industry).
2. The company must be heavily invested in by individuals and in- stitutions (high numbers of outstanding shares).
3. The company is not a transportation or utility company (they have their own averages).
4. The company must have an excellent reputation (this is open to interpretation).

Changes are seldom made and generally occur when the fundamentals of a company have shifted dramatically. When this happens all stocks in the average are evaluated, which is why we see changes occurring in multiples, such as the latest in November 1999 when four stocks were removed from the DJIA and replaced by four different stocks.

THE STANDARD & POOR'S 500 INDEX

Many felt that Dow's method of calculation was outdated because each of the 30 companies is equal in basis and the size of a company or its capitalization (stock price multiplied by number of outstanding shares) is not considered a factor. A newer criticism is that the Dow's core 30 stocks do not reflect a complete picture of the stock market today. It's important for the individual investor to compare their portfolios to other more complete indexes.

COMPARE ALCOA AND IBM in Table 2.1. You see that Alcoa's price is far lower than IBM's, for instance. Yet, they have the same impact when calculating the average because they are weighted based on stock price. When the price of IBM goes up or down, however, it can have a greater overall effect on the Index than Alcoa stock.

In response to these criticisms, additional indexes were created.

The Standard & Poor's 500 Index dates back to 1923, when the index consisted of 233 companies and 26 industries. By 1957, the S&P expanded to 500 companies and has grown to include some 90 industries, covering the major sectors of industrials, utilities, financials, and transportation. There is no set number of companies in a sector. Back in 1988, the S&P Index Committee created a "float" situation to allow them to react more quickly to market dynamics. The stocks covered by the S&P 500 Index are traded on the NYSE, American Stock Exchange (AMEX), and the NASDAQ. Selection to the S&P 500 is based on the importance of companies to the U.S. economy and is not solely dependent on sales, capitalization (size), or profits (e.g., DJIA blue chips). Many, of course, are leaders in their industries. Companies cannot apply to the S&P Committee for selection since all decisions are made based on company fundamentals, which is information available to the public. Guidelines for adding stocks to the S&P 500 Index are:

1. Market Value: companies selected have the largest market value in their industry (outstanding shares times stock price).

2. Industry Group Classification: companies representing important industries within the U.S. economy.

3. Capitalization: companies that are widely held by the public.

4. Trading Activity: companies who have ample liquidity and share pricing.

5. Fundamentals: companies that are financially stable and operate efficiently.

6. Emerging Industries: companies in new industry groups must meet the same guidelines as above.

The S&P 500 is capitalization weighted (each company's outstanding shares multiplied by its stock price), making each company's influence on the Index performance directly proportional to that company's size (number of outstanding shares). Compare that to the DJIA which only measures average price movement of a stock and each stock is valued the same in the Index. On the S&P 500 a large change in the price of one company will not affect the outcome of the index as greatly as it would on the DJIA. Because of this, the U.S. Department of Commerce regarded the S&P 500 a better indicator of the nation's economy and listed it with its Index of Leading Economic Indicators in 1968.

The S&P 500 also addressed the needs of the professionals. Because the S&P 500 measures the performance of a major portion of the U.S. stock market, professionals could now use this benchmark to compare their stock portfolios. The smart investor can use this as a guideline for his own portfolio.

WHY DO COMPANIES get removed from the S&P 500? There are four main reasons: merger with, or acquisition by, another company, restructuring, financial failure, or lack of representation.

NASDAQ-100 INDEX

The NASDAQ-100 Index is considered the index for the new economy stocks. Since its inception in 1985, it has been comprised mostly of the largest, most actively traded technology stocks (computer hardware and software, telecommunications, and biotechnology), and a sprinkling of retail, manufacturing, and service companies. For many it represents the future growth of America. The NASDAQ-100, an index that parallels the activity of the Nasdaq Exchange, has shown a growth burst of nearly 3000% since the inception (figure as of 6/30/00) of some of the largest growth companies (non-financial) listed on the NASDAQ. The index's guide for selection is that a company must have a minimum market capitalization of $500 million, have an intensive daily trading volume of at least 100,000 shares, and be listed on the NASDAQ for at least two years.

STARTING IN 1998, non-U.S. companies listed on the Nasdaq Exchange were included in the NASDAQ-100 Index.

As if that weren't enough, because of the immense growth in the Nasdaq, in 1999 it introduced a way for individual investors to own a piece of the NASDAQ-100 Index—the Nasdaq 100 Index Tracking Stock (Amex: QQQ)—a stock with the characteristics of a mutual fund. This is a boon for the investor. Now you can own more than a few tech stocks or a managed limited mutual fund. You can own 100 tech stocks by owning shares in the QQQ.

A NASDAQ ticker symbol is recognized as having four or five letters. Less than four letters (one, two, or three) indicates a NYSE listing.

THE NASDAQ COMPOSITE INDEX

At the other end of the spectrum is the Nasdaq Composite Index, which includes over 5,300 companies trading on the Nasdaq Exchange. The index calculates market value (last sale price multiplied by total shares outstanding) throughout the trading day to continually monitor fluctuations of all domestic and foreign stocks listed on the Nasdaq. This comprehensive, broad-based index is also divided into eight industry-specific indexes for banks, biotechnology, computer, finance, industrial, insurance, telecommunications, and transportation stocks. Essentially, it gives a continual picture of all the Nasdaq stocks.

OTHER INDEXES

The more stocks there are, the more indexes will be devised. Other indexes worth noting are the Wilshire 5000, which actually contains more than 7,000 issued stocks, and the Russell 2000, a comprehensive look at U.S. small cap companies ranging in value from $58 million to $600 million. Other indexes include: Russell 1000, Russell 3000, S&P Midcap, S&P 100, and Value Line Composite. Non-U.S. indexes of importance are: CAC-40 (France), DAX (Germany), FTSE-100 (Great Britain), and Nikkei (Japan).

The important thing to remember is that all of the indexes are tools by which we can assess the market's movement. We can track our own portfolios in much the same way on a daily, weekly, monthly (but preferably quarterly basis) simply by comparing the rate of change in our portfolio with any of the indexes to see if our stock portfolios are even with, falling below, or beating the index.

Together with the DOW, S&P offers the investor a significantly wider view in choosing stocks to buy or sell. Becoming familiar with these two indexes will raise the odds for successful investments. Additionally, the economic indicators listed in the next chapter, when compared to the indexes, offer deeper wisdom to all investors, beginners to advanced.

CHAPTER THREE

Back to Basics—The ABCs of Investing

KEY TERMS

- AAII (American Association of Individual Investors)
  An educational and resource organization for investors.
- Blue Chip
  Stocks of seasoned companies that represent relatively conservative and low-risk investments.
- bulls and bears
  A shorthand way to describe a market where prices are moving upward (bulls) or downward (bears).
- dollar cost averaging
  Investing in a company in regular intervals to help lower the average cost per share.
- DRIPs (Dividend Reinvestment Programs)
  Company programs that automatically reinvest a shareholder's dividends into more shares of the company's stock.
- NAIC (National Association of Investors Clubs)
  An educational and resource organization for investor clubs and individuals.
- price-to-earnings ratio or P/E
  The ratio of a company's stock price per share to its earnings.
- Value Line
  Investment survey—a resource for researching stocks.

While writing my first book, the financially based lifestyle book *You've Earned It, Don't Lose It*, with personal finance guru Suze Orman, we discussed investing at great length. The one point she made that has always stayed with me is that I potentially know as much about a company as any stockbroker. At the time, I understood intellectually what she meant, but it wasn't until a remarkable sequence of events occurred that the truth rang clear. Willing to put this philosophy to the test, I began to flex my investing muscles. I asked a broker to purchase shares of a particular retail company for me. I shopped at this nationally known high-end retail cookware company, as well as its other divisions, and knew they were also successful in direct mail. Not too long after, this same broker approached me with a public offering of another retail company I also knew. He gave me his one-minute spiel about the store's radical new marketing concept and merchandising approach, after which I explained to him that not only was I aware of the company, but I also knew about its competition and shortcomings. I politely declined the offer and further remarked that the company would not be around in a year. It turned out that I was right and that launched me into becoming an independent investor. That bit of knowledge was my salvation. Later I realized that Suze was both right *and* wrong in her original statement. I didn't know as much as the broker, I knew more. He was merely a salesman peddling his wares with no real understanding of what he was selling. I was out in the trenches. Confidence in hand, I opened a self-directed brokerage account with Charles Schwab & Company.

At almost the same time, the Beardstown Ladies exploded on the scene with their first book, *The Beardstown Ladies' Common Sense Investment Guide*, bringing the National Association of Investors Clubs (NAIC) into the spotlight. I now embarked on an educational journey. As an investor, you have probably already heard what the basic rules of investing are, but they're worth repeating.

Here are seven basic rules every investor should never circumvent when considering buying a stock:

Getting Started

1. Investigate a company before buying

Building Your Portfolio

2. Buy growth stocks

3. Look for companies that are well-managed

4. Buy when the price is right

5. Diversify your portfolio

Maintaining Your Portfolio

6. Invest for the long term

7. Invest regularly and reinvest dividends

Try as we might, it's hard to stick to these basic investing principles when the market is in a frenzied upswing. But it's for this very reason that we have to make an agreement with ourselves and stick to a smart investing plan, *before* the bottom falls out.

Rule 1: Let's begin with what should be your mantra: I will *investigate* thoroughly before investing in any company. A good company is going to be around for a long time, so there is no need to feel panicked and rushed to buy. Don't be an emotional buyer and over-react like my friend's sister who got caught up in the Amazon.com bubble. *"Can you believe what Amazon is up to? I just bought some."* Without researching the company and understanding that such prices cannot be sustained when a company isn't profitable, she threw her money at Amazon, buying at a high price. The rest as they say is history.

All companies have a past worth scrutinizing and their history is part of the public record. A company should have at least a five-year history for you to compare; all of this information is readily available on the web, in Value Line, or in the company's annual report. But don't stop there. Avail yourself of the company's latest news. All companies are in the news, even if only to announce their quarterly earnings. Also, a company with a solid foundation can sustain bumpy weather following some bad news, such as a recall or litigation. Johnson & Johnson's dramatic stock drop after the Tylenol murders in October 1982 is an example.

As we mentioned in the preceding chapter, begin to understand how the economy affects the stock market and its various industries. Read the business news about the economy and pay attention to how the news affects the stock market. For instance, what happens to the market when the jobless rate increases? Decreases? We will cover more about economic indicators in Chapter 6.

VALUE LINE (found in your library's reference section) is a particularly good resource for an on-the-spot analysis because it helps to answer several of our previous questions regarding a company's fundamentals. Ask your librarian for the schematic called "Getting The Most From The Value Line Page." It explains the different sections on the page.

BUILDING YOUR PORTFOLIO

Rule 2: Look for companies that offer growth and value. Now you have to do your homework, which is painstaking, but necessary for earning an "A+" in investing. Growth and value are determined by increased profitability, increased earnings, and increased dividends (if divs are paid). If these factors are positive over a five-year period, there's a good chance this is a sustainable, growing company. Companies that have sustained an annual growth of 10% or more over a five-year period have a solid growth history.

To begin to get a sense of growth and value, look at any chart that depicts historic sales, earnings, and stock price. NAIC has a worksheet that they call the Stock Selection Guide (SSG), which readily shows the relationship of these three factors to each other. The theory is that sales drive earnings and earnings drive price. A company that cannot increase its sales and earnings will not increase in share price or value. When looking for value companies, focus on companies that are at the top in their industry, and who have strong competitive positions.

Rule 3: Look for companies that are well-managed. Jason B. broke this cardinal rule of investing when he bought a well-known computer tech stock on a tip. Had he looked into the company before leaping, he would have discovered that during its new regime it was losing market share and sales. News was rampant about the CEO being pushed out and the company was not positioned for growth. These were all clear signs of mismanagement.

Rule 4: Playing "The Price is Right." When trying to evaluate whether a stock is reasonably priced for purchase, one thing we can do is look at its price to earnings ratio or P/E (the stock's recent price divided by its last 12 months of reported earnings)—sometimes referred to as "times earnings." P/Es can be found in the stock market section of the newspaper and can change daily as the price of the stock changes. The P/E ratio is an indicator of the market's enthusiasm for a stock, or what investors are willing to pay for the stock. You can determine if this is high (overvalued—a very enthusiastic market willing to overpay) or low (undervalued—a dulled, unresponsive market; investors hate the stock) by applying several factors. First, look at the P/E ratios for the past five years and average them. If the current P/E is within or below that range, this suggests the stock may be priced reasonably for purchase. If you cannot find historical P/Es, you can go to the company's Value Line page, find the line called "Avg Ann'l P/E Ratio" (see Figure 3.1) and use these numbers to add and divide, or simply look at the top bar on the Value Line page. Next to the P/E ratio (current), in parentheses, is the Median P/E for the past ten years. If the current P/E is higher than the median, you are looking at an overpriced stock.

Let's look at my Intel stock for January 2000. At the "closing bell" on January 14, 2000, before the stock split, Intel was selling for just over $103 per share. Its "current" P/E ratio was just above 40, but its "median" P/E as seen in Value Line (remember that's a ten-year average) was only 13. Overvalued.

Now let's look at the ramifications of buying an overvalued stock despite continuous growth in earnings and dividends. In 1973, Coca-Cola was selling at 42 times earnings (price to earnings ratio of 42). If you had purchased the stock at this high, you would not have made money on your investment for 13 years even though earnings and dividends tripled between 1973 and 1986.[1]

---

[1] Investment Quarterly, *The Atlanta Journal Constitution*, January 3, 2000.

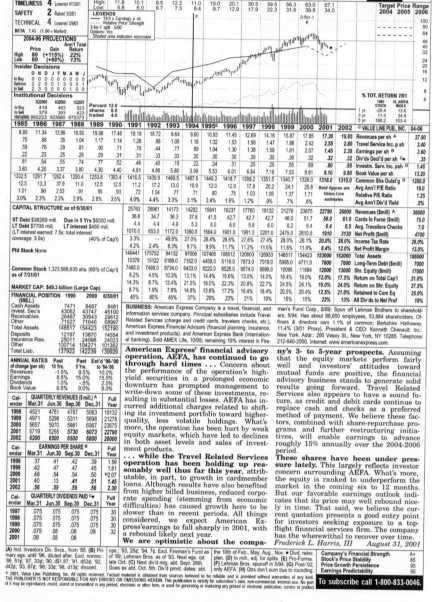

FIGURE 3.1   American Express Value Linepage.

W HEN YOU SEE A STOCK with no price-to-earnings ratio, remember this means that the company *has no earnings* (see Lucent, May 2001, for example).

Investigation into a company can determine why investors feel positive or negative about the company. The P/E ratio is one very important factor. The bottom line is: make sure that your decision to buy is based on good solid fundamentals and not market frenzy.

Rule 5: Diversify your portfolio. Not all companies grow at the same rate and have the same risk factors. A large-cap, or Blue Chip, stock does not grow as rapidly year after year as a small or mid-sized growth company does. To maintain a portfolio of strictly large cap stocks will generally render less risk, but also less return. When you diversify your portfolio—that is, divide your holdings among large, mid-size, and small companies—you can achieve the goal of doubling your portfolio's value in five, seven, or ten years. This mix of holdings also balances your portfolio's risk (think of it as the "not putting all of your eggs in one basket" theory of investing). As an investor, you will have to take the risk litmus test and determine your personal "risk quotient." Based on such factors as your age, how long you have been investing, how nervous the market's ups and downs make you, and so on, you must decide what portfolio mix of small, mid-cap, and large-cap companies is best for you. The NAIC traditionally offers these market capitalization (total market value) ranges for small-, mid-, and large-cap companies:

Small-Cap: $50 million to $200 million

Mid-Cap: $200 million to $1.5 billion

Large-Cap: $1.5 billion or more

MAINTAINING YOUR PORTFOLIO

Rule 6: Buy for the long term. We have all heard about day-traders, individuals who buy a stock one hour and sell it the next, seeking profit from any jump in price. This is a game of "one step forward and two steps back," risky at best and disastrous at its worst as portrayed in the

2000 movie *Rogue Trader*. For every gain the day-trader makes, there are fees to be paid on both ends of the deal, buying and selling. Even with reduced on-line broker fees, the increase in the stock's price would have to be enormous to realize profits at the end of the day. And any monies made are generally put back into buying another stock to begin the process all over again. Long-term investing in solid growth companies can double your money every five years *if* you maintain a portfolio with a minimum 15% annual growth rate. With a 10% annual compounded growth rate, you can double your money every seven years (or quadruple it in 15 years).

Rule 7: Invest on a regular basis and reinvest dividends. It doesn't take a lot of money to make money. To begin investing today you can purchase as little as a single share of a stock. Through educational associations like NAIC and AAII (American Association of Individual Investors), and through companies like First Share you can purchase a single share of a company's stock (you will pay the stock price at the time purchase is made plus a processing fee). Once purchased, an account is set up in your name directly with that company (its bank or plan administrator). You can continue to invest any amount (mostly at a $25 minimum) at any time to buy shares or fractions of shares, thus building your holding in that company. These direct investment accounts are called DRIPs (Dividend Reinvestment Programs) and are only available from companies that pay dividends. Dripping means that when the company pays its quarterly dividend, that amount of money, however small it may seem, stays in your account and is used to purchase additional portions of the stock. Here's an example: I bought one share of Intel at $68 on May 22, 1996. When the company paid its first dividend on September 3, 1996, in the amount of $.05 per share, my 1 share now became 1.0006 shares. Each time a dividend was paid, this number of shares (or fraction) increased. So even if I never put another dime into buying another share, my holdings in that company would continue to grow through dividend reinvestment (and stock splits, if there are any).

A SINGLE SHARE of a stock makes a great gift that can keep on giving.

DOLLAR COST AVERAGING

Reinvesting on a regular basis gives you what is commonly referred to as "dollar cost averaging." As an example, if you purchase a stock when the price is $10 a share, buy again when the price is $12, then again at $14, when you add these prices and divide by the number of times you invested (in this case three), you have paid an average price of $12 per share for the stock, even though it is already valued at $14. You are already ahead of the game.

THE DOW THEORY OF MARKET MOVEMENT

Early in Charles Dow's journalism career covering the stock market, he began to report on market behaviors that he observed. Though he never named the theory after himself, it has remained the basis of how the market is viewed. Analysts synthesized the information down to a few essential points.

MARKET MOVEMENT

The market reveals three types of movements: *Primary*, or large movements that take place over the course of years; *secondary* movements that take place over the course of weeks or months that run contrary to the primary trend; and *daily* market fluctuations that may run in either direction. As such, these daily fluctuations tend to be less important individually, but they are important in that they are part of the overall trend.

INDICATORS

The Industrial Average and the Transportation Average must support each other's direction because as different and independent industry sectors, they rely heavily on one another. In other words, industrials rely on transportation to get their product to market. When industrials do well, so should transportation. It is when we see one sector pulling ahead and doing better than the other without the other sector catching up that an indication of a major reversal in the market is beginning to take place. This means we may be moving from an upward trend market (bull) to a downward trend market (bear) or vice versa, depending on the indicators. To be a savvy investor, it is important to understand the signals.

THE BULLS AND THE BEARS

We hear a lot about the bull and bear markets—and that bull is good and bear is not. But, each has distinctive stages it plays out and recognizing these stages may be essential to your investment strategy.

Running with the Bulls

In a sequence of events not unlike the Annual Running of the Bulls in Pamplona, Spain, the first phase of a bull market is referred to as the *accumulation* phase. *Think of this as the time when all the bulls are gathered from all over the country, months in advance of the event.* Stock market prices are depressed and are supported by gloomy financial reports. *Think of this as the weather report forecasting gloomy weather for the big day in Pamplona.* It is the farsighted investor, however, who uses this period of depressed prices to buy shares. *He's checking the long-term weather reports, buying several types of gear, and making his plane reservation for Pamplona.*

The second phase of a bull market is the *big buzz*. There is increased activity, rising prices, and better financial reports (*prerunning of the bulls hype*). Large gains are made; some stocks are touted as "hot"; Wall Street is running on high adrenalin (*the bets are on the table*). We hear all about the big money being made. But how long can this be sustained before there is a reversal?

Meeting the Bears

The bulls are now released into the narrow streets of Pamplona. As a compact, tight-knit group, they are a killing-machine. Now begins the first phase of the bear market, the *distribution phase. Those bulls on the streets of Pamplona are beginning to scatter and thin out and are no longer as powerful.* The uninformed knee-jerk investor is just now jumping into the ring (*placing his bets or jumping into the street to show his bravado*), while the informed investor sees the scramble and begins to sell shares. Now we have an oversupply of shares in the marketplace. Oversupply brings prices down and makes profits even harder to come by.

So starts phase two of the bear market: *panic selling.* People see prices spiraling downward at nearly the same pace they shot up and they begin to sell off their holdings, kicking off phase three of the bear market: *further weakening and erosion of prices.* Those issues we once thought of as "hot" have all but erased previous bull market gains and the news is nothing but gloom and doom.

The moral of this story: just remember that they will run those bulls through the streets of Pamplona again. Preparation is the key.

SOME BULL and bear highlights: 1954–1969 saw our first big bull market mostly due to the post-war economic prosperity of the 1950s. The 1970s' bear market was sparked by oil problems and currency devaluation. The 1980s' bull run was backed by junk bonds and a propensity for mergers. On October 19, 1987, "Black Monday" saw a 23% drop in the Dow only to see the market back on its feet one year later, ushering in the 1990s' technology boom, Internet and dotcom mania, and ultra high P/Es. The 21st century? Well, that still remains to be seen.

Ultimately, researching the histories and financials of the giant "blue chip" stocks may teach us a lesson about building and maintaining a balanced portfolio, as we will see in the next chapters.

CHAPTER FOUR

The Annual Report— Part 1: Using the Annual Report

KEY TERMS

- annual report
  The report a company publishes for its stockholders at the end of each fiscal year, reporting on its financial condition and significant events.

- GAAP (generally accepted accounting principles)
  A set of rules and reporting guidelines companies must follow to present financial information.

- 10-K
  A financial report that the Securities and Exchange Commission requires companies to submit yearly, containing more detailed financial information than the annual report.

MY TOUGHEST TASK as an individual investor was to learn how to "read" an annual report (AR). Each spring a daunting number of annual report books and supplements would show up, only to be set aside with the intention that they would be read. Eventually they were just thrown into the recycling bin. In time, I realized that the annual report is completely manageable if broken down into its components.

WHAT IS AN ANNUAL REPORT?

A company's annual report is just that: a report made on an annual basis to the shareholders of the company, informing them, both descriptively and in numbers, of what the company has accomplished during the previous year. This report is mandated by the federal government and required to include certain information and financial data. It is also filed with the federal government in the no-glitz form referred to as a 10-K. This is a report filed with the SEC (Securities and Exchange Commission) within 90 days after the close of the company's fiscal year and generally contains even more fiscal information than the annual report. You can access the 10-K reports online at *www.edgar-online.com* or *www.freeedgar.com*.

Within the pages of the annual report there is valuable information that can be gleaned and it comes in the form of both biased (subjective) and impartial (objective) information. Subjectively, the company can legitimately put its best foot forward in whatever interpretive dance it sees fit—from photos of smiling faces, to products leaping across the page, to the Chairman's/CEO's Letter to the Shareholders—information to share, but not mandated by the SEC. Objectively, the information has to be truthful, so companies must follow specific guidelines as set forth by the SEC.

We'll begin with an overview of the various sections of the report, followed by the best way to approach a report, formulas to help interpret the information, and fill-in charts to help you understand a company.

DISSECTING THE ANNUAL REPORT SECTION BY SECTION

The annual report can be divided into optional and SEC-mandated information.

Optional Information

The point of looking at the optional material is to see what is and isn't there. Has the company addressed problems head on or chosen to ignore them in the Statement or Letter to Shareholders, for instance?

- Financial Highlights—Drawn from the consolidated financial pages, this page offers an overview of the company's financials.
- Letter to Shareholders—The Chairman or CEO says "hi" and "this is how we did last year."
- Business Review—Here's where the company tells you about its business, part by part.
- Board of Directors and Management (usually found in the back)—Who runs the company and makes decisions.
- Stockholder Information (usually found in the back)—Who to call, where to write.

SEC-Mandated Information

- Financial data: Balance sheet, income statement, statement of cash flow.
- Management Report—A discussion about the company's financial condition based on the numbers on the following pages.
- Auditor's Report—The auditor is an independent company that goes over the books to make sure everything is on the up-and-up.
- Company Report on Financial Statements—The company's sworn statement that it didn't fudge.
- Financial statements and notes (footnotes—usually found near the back)—The detailed explanations of information on the preceding pages. Some call this section "the dirty laundry."

THE OPTIONAL MATERIAL

Financial Highlights

Generally preceding the Letter to the Shareholders, this page or two has colorful graphs, charts, and lists offering an overview of the company's products or divisions and their revenues. This is a good place to see a two- to three-year comparison of some of the financial particulars from the financial review section. For instance, in 1999, Philip

Morris's AR clearly shows that the mainstay of their revenue is from tobacco, more from international sales than domestic, but a major portion of total sales nonetheless, considering that they also owned
domestic and international food and beer operations at the time.

Intel's 1999 AR offers financial bar graphs and a pie chart indicating the geographic breakdown of revenues. It is interesting to note
that all of the financial bar graphs are aligned (net revenues, diluted
earnings per share, stock price trading ranges, R&D, book value per
share) except for Return on Average Shareholder's Equity (though
their percentages were still pretty high). This snapshot also offers
the percentage change from the previous year. It is easy to determine
this change: When viewing the financial highlights, compare one
year to the next to get a much fuller picture of a company's growth
(or decline).

Letter to the Shareholders

Here the CEO or Chairman of the company paints a picture of the previous year. In broad, sweeping strokes he or she discusses the company's overall performance, its challenges and goals. Because the
letter is written in plain English (and it should be) doesn't mean that
it is fully understandable. You will have to become an interpreter (critical reader) and learn to read between the lines. So, with yellow
marker in hand, along with a red pen, let's focus on certain language
and phrases to be on the lookout for.

- Strong, positive, forceful language and active verbs.

  In its 2000 annual report, Johnson & Johnson cautions against
  any forward-looking statements by saying that things can
  change. They identify words like plan, expect, will, anticipate,
  estimate, and so on. Others are: believe, intend, project.

- Specific numbers.

- Vague phrases that appear to be nothing more than hype or
  fluff, in other words, where nothing much is being said or
  backed up with an action plan. Here are two examples of
  vague statements.

—"To achieve a superior return on investment, we will be prudent in our investment decisions." —Newell Rubbermaid, 2000 annual report, pages 2,3.

—". . . committed enormous resources on a variety of fronts." —Philip Morris Companies, Inc., 1999 annual report, page 4.

- Statements that sound overly optimistic.

- Apologies for missing any of their goals and why.

- Circuitous reasoning.

The language used in the Letter to the Shareholders may portend what to expect in the rest of the annual report.

The Business Review or Corporate Message

Because this isn't a mandated portion of the annual report, companies use this to dramatize their business. You will get a good sense of how a company *wants to be viewed*: everything about their products, services, and objectives is covered in this section of the report. Recent trends, developments, and acquisitions are also covered. When you go through this section, especially for companies that manufacture goods, you will be amazed at what you don't know. For example, did you know that Kraft Foods (Philip Morris as of 2001) has a licensing agreement with Starbucks to bring their coffee brand into supermarkets? That Johnson & Johnson isn't just powder for a baby's bottom or Band-Aids for boo-boos, but also includes the French skin care sensation RoC Anti-wrinkle cream you may have seen advertised on TV? That Coca-Cola partnered with Warner Brothers to produce the Harry Potter films? As an investor, you should have keen knowledge of the company, and its products and services.

The company's sales and marketing should be included. From this, you will get a sense of what the company sells, or the services it provides, to whom they offer this product or service, how they sell their product or service, and where it is sold. Generally, too, where they can point out increased sales, they offer up a comparison with the previous year.

Board of Directors and Management

This section is usually located at the back of the annual report. The names and positions of the directors and top management team are listed here. What you won't see here that you do see in the accompanying tissue-thin "Notice of Stockholders Meeting and Proxy Statement," are salaries, bonuses, and other monetary compensation they receive for doing their jobs, the number of shares of stock each owns (including any shares owned by spouses and children), and exercisable and unexercisable security options. This is important to note because you want to know what percentage of stock insiders own. Insider information can also be obtained on the Value Line page (See Figure 3.1 in Chapter 3).

Stockholder Information

This section is usually located at the back of the annual report. Here's where you find the address of the company headquarters and division headquarters, if any, website access information, stock exchange listing, annual meeting date, time and place, shareholder services and transfer agents (for Dividend Reinvestment Plans) and any additional information the company thinks is necessary, pertinent, or will fill up the page.

SEC-MANDATED MATERIALS

Now we get to the heart of the annual report, the straightforward information that the government requires in every annual report.

Report of Management

Unlike the corporate message, this is a serious statement regarding the veracity of the financial information, their internal controls for reporting this information, and their compliance with government regulations and federal laws. This is pretty much a cookie-cutter statement.

Auditors' Report

This report is generated by an independent accounting firm and states that the financial data is complete and has been prepared in accordance with generally accepted accounting principles (GAAP). If anything extraordinary shows up it is addressed with management prior to the filing of the 10-K and the production of the annual report so that changes or explanations can be made. If reparation hasn't been made, the auditors' report will state any irregularities.

Management Discussion

The company's performance is analyzed for results of operations and financial condition (how much liquid and capital resources they have to fund those operations). Look for two-year comparisons here, along with any statement of varying accounting standards and practices, and pending litigation.

Financial Statements and Notes

The numbers tell the whole story: they verify the company's recent financial history and how well it performed. The SEC requires that only three statements be published by the company: statement of earnings, statement of financial position (the Balance Sheet), and statement of cash flows. But no less important to understand is the rest of the financial data, including the statement of stockholders' equity and the page of selected financial data.

APPROACHING AN ANNUAL REPORT—CULLING FOR INFORMATION

Though we dissect the report section by section for pertinent information, it is often said that you should read an annual report backwards, starting with the notes or footnotes. This is where a company keeps its dirty laundry. And even though this is just part of your research into a company, in the notes you will find out instantly if there are any problems or deviations. But more about footnotes later.

Let's take a look at the 1999 and 2000 annual reports for Philip Morris Companies, Inc. This is merely an example to follow and in no way serves as a recommendation for stock purchase. You can view the annual report online at *www.philipmorris.com*, but we will provide portions of the financial data.

The Cover

This 1999 full-color book printed on heavy stock depicts nine smiling men and an equal number of women of all ethnicities (and nationalities as noted on page 18 of the report). The lower band of the cover is a line-up of Philip Morris products along with the slogan "Working to make a difference. The People of Philip Morris." The 2000 annual report shows no people and no tobacco products (on the online version) because "it is not [their] intention to market, advertise or promote our cigarette brands on this site."

Inside Front Cover

Here's where we learn what the slogan means. They are putting money behind a campaign to communicate who they are or who they would like us to think they are, depending on your point of view. It's a brief, carefully crafted statement. Interestingly, though we know that Philip Morris manufactures tobacco among other things at this time, there is never the mention of the word "tobacco" in this message—although it clearly accounts for the major part of their revenue as we will see. If you look at the 2000 annual report for Johnson & Johnson (which is one of my holdings), there are no prosaic advertising statements even though they, too, are involved in various product and patent litigations.

Financial Highlights

All of the numbers are stated in millions of dollars, except for per share data—no point in wasting all those zeros. Everyone does it this way. But it should be noted that the number you are reading at the top (revenues) is 78 *billion*, five hundred and ninety six million (refer to page 1 of the online 2000 annual report). Anything displaying over three digits is read in the billions. Three digits and under is read as millions. Also, all of this information is presented elsewhere in the report so you needn't spend much time here, but it gives a good overview: two-year comparisons, growth rates dating back to 1984, and results by segment. Johnson & Johnson, on the other hand, does not offer as extensive an overview by including results by segment, but the three-year comparison (many companies will offer up to eleven years of information) is in plainer English. Instead of referring to Operating Revenues, which means revenues or sales, JNJ simply calls it "sales to customers." What's more interesting to note are the footnotes at the bottom of the page that offer a brief explanation of results. Let's move on.

Letter to Shareowners

Putting the company's best foot forward is the purpose of the letter to shareholders. Owners of a company want to hear good news from the head of the company, but they also want explanations about what went wrong during the past year and how it will be corrected. It is always interesting to read and compare with previous years to see if the company has maintained its business philosophy, if any changes occurred in management, what problems they may have endured, and what goals and commitments they plan for the future.

Overall, the message should be straightforward. Philip Morris tells us right from the get-go that litigation and price increases due to the Master Settlement Agreement in 1998, as well as the economic downturn, were major problems for the company. The stock lost 78% of its value, yet they were still able to increase Earnings Per Share. In 2000 they mention that they once again faced an unfavorable currency impact (currency exchange rate on foreign sales). But instead of telling the shareholder what he/she did earn, CEO Geoffrey C. Bible offers up what would have been (you can find earnings on the Financial Highlights page. Answer: 12.4%). Not included in the income statement for the year because the acquisition came in December 1999, but highlighted in the Letter, is Philip Morris's acquisition of Nabisco to its Kraft food group, which made them the second largest food company in the world. Next year's report should be interesting, given the spin-off of Kraft Foods. CEO Bible tells us the cost of the acquisition, the increased performance of Nabisco in 2000 (even though it doesn't go to Philip Morris's bottom line), and what worldwide revenues "would have been" if combined with Kraft's bottom line.

I always find it interesting to look for non-specific terminology like "finished the year with strong momentum"(Philip Morris 1999 annual report, page 2) or "would have been" (Philip Morris 1999 annual report, pp. 2 and 4) or "committed enormous resources on a variety of fronts" (Philip Morris 1999 annual report, p. 4). So, look for what the company "did" instead of shoulda', coulda' and woulda' in these reports. To its benefit, Philip Morris did meet its growth target, offering its 33rd dividend increase in 31 years. They also gave us a projected growth target of 13% to 15%.

Remember when I mentioned that the cover didn't include photos of smiling faces on the 2000 annual report? Well, they covered their bases on page 2 in the letter "To Our Shareholders." Toward the end of the page, they relate the percentage of "people of color" and women there is in their workforce, including a management breakdown. They must have a better PR team because this wasn't addressed in their 1999 report. Do you think perhaps they had more women doing their PR in 2000?

This said, remember it's just a way to help promote the company and not SEC required information. It's where the investor can get a feel for how the company wants to be perceived.

The Business Review

Same information, more detail by product-segment. But some interesting tidbits can be gathered. In 1999, Philip Morris began phasing out its Louisville Tobacco plant. In 1999 they refer to the number of cigarettes shipped, whereas in 2000 they are referred to as "units." In 1999 they mingled societal concerns (youth smoking prevention, regulation of cigarettes, etc.) with new marketing initiatives (Party at the Ranch Sweepstakes). In 2000 societal concerns are addressed separately and a dollar amount is attached to their Youth Smoking Prevention program.

Corporate citizenship or commitment to the community bodes well for companies these days. Whether or not to address corporate giving in the annual report is optional. Obviously, if a company needs to be viewed in a better light, they will report on all the ways they try to make a difference through programs and funding. Johnson & Johnson and Coca-Cola, for instance, don't make multi-page references to their service to the community in their annual reports, but both companies post on their websites extensive materials relating to their worldwide contributions and community programs.

When you compare a company's annual report year-to-year or compare its style to other companies, you get a fuller understanding of how the annual report is utilized by the company. But, the telltale information is in the financials and as we delve into this in the next chapter, we will have some equations to work.

CHAPTER FIVE

The Annual Report— Part 2: The Financials

KEY TERMS

- asset/equity ratio
  Total assets divided by shareholder equity.

- capital structure
  The long-term financing of a company, including long-term debt, common stock and preferred stock, and retained earnings.

- debt/equity ratio
  A measure of a company's leverage or degree to which they are using borrowed money calculated by dividing long-term debt by common shareholders' equity.

- equity
  Ownership interest in a company in the form of common stock or preferred stock. Total assets minus total liabilities; also called shareholder's equity or net worth or book value.

- par value
  The indicated price of a share of stock should the company go under.

Iknow it may seem daunting at first, but don't skip the financial information in an annual report. Along with the ratios and charts we will be providing, this information is the foundation of your research into any company. So, we will approach it section by section.

MANAGEMENT'S DISCUSSION AND ANALYSIS OF FINANCIAL CONDITION AND RESULTS OF OPERATION

This is a mouthful, but the SEC requires this (M D & A) commentary and though it is not formulaic and may not appear the same from one company report to another, the information is basically the same: A general statement about the business, results of operations, liquidity and capital resources. Some of the information in these sections includes:

- assessment graph or summary of products, including new product launches and past product problems
- sales and earnings including net earnings; costs and expenses, the impact of foreign currency exchange rates
- profit by product segment; some may be given by geographic breakdowns as well
- liquidity and cash resources
- new accounting procedures, stock process, dividends (if any)
- a caution against any forward-looking statements which says that things may happen that could change the results of a company's expectations and projections. JNJ identifies these forward-looking statements in their 2000 annual report, as discussed in the previous chapter. And if the change factors they are talking about are not discussed in this section, as they are by Philip Morris, they can be seen in the company's 10-K filing.

THE FINANCIAL STATEMENTS

Now, let's explore the financial data. When you look at the financial statements in this second section of the annual report, you will see that they are referred to as "consolidated." This simply means that all of the company's data from all of its subsidiaries, foreign and domestic, are added together—consolidated—into one report. Sometimes we see a chart called "Selected Financial Data" that gives us a three- to ten-year overview. Here's something I like to do when there is a financial review chart: I look at the numbers on each line over the past five years and make little arrows indicating a continual increase (up arrow), decrease (down arrow), or no movement (sideways arrow).

For example: the Philip Morris annual report 2000, page 33, presents a five-year summary of operations chart (as compared to AR 1999, which shows eleven years). The very first line, operating revenues (how much money they brought in), quite obviously shows a steady increase over the past five years. So, I would place an *up* arrow next to the most recent column. I go through each line of significance and place an arrow up, down, or sideways. Note in particular the lines for sales (revenue), cost of sales, research & development expenses, earnings per share, dividends declared, dividends as % of EPS, long-term debt and price-to-earnings ratio. As we move down the rows, look at the line that indicates "total debt." Notice anything significant about the recent number? Philip Morris's total debt for 2000 doubled from 1999. When you read through the M D & A, look for reasons for this increase in debt. Page 26 indicates $9.2 billion was borrowed to help acquire Nabisco. Reading further down, notice that the IPO (initial public offering, and not considered a spin-off by the Company) of Kraft Foods will help pay down some of that debt.

Consolidated Statements of Earnings (or Income)

This is the numerical explanation of gross sales (revenues) for a company and what the company ends up with after expenses are deducted (operating income) and taxes paid. This leftover money is called *earnings* or *net income* or *profit*. This chart also covers the company's performance over the entire year. One question to ask as you begin is: where did the earnings come from? It is important that earnings come from sales and not from cutbacks or sell-offs. The footnotes should provide answers.

Philip Morris's expenses for 2000 decreased, creating an increased bottom line (the earnings). But notice that they haven't paid out any litigation settlements for the years 1999 and 2000. Will this continue? Again, see the notes regarding litigation cases. You can also learn more by listening to the most recent call report on Morningstar.com.

Basically the figures on this chart show a company's capability of making a profit. This statement can indicate trends in revenue, operating income, and gross profit margins. Here's an explanation of what you will see and a ratio for calculating return on equity.

Sales, *revenues*, and *operating revenues* are the same thing: It's what the company makes for selling their product or service. Philip Morris refers to this as Operating Revenues. Just look for the words "sales" or "revenues" on the top line.

Gross profit is what they receive after deducting the "cost of sales" or the cost of materials and manufacturing that go into making the final products.

Operating income is what the company gets after the cost of doing business is deducted. The cost of doing business includes such expenses as administration, advertising, salaries, research and development, rents, and so on. Add or deduct any additional income or loss to the company through investments, and you get *income before taxes*.

Net income or *net earnings* is after-tax money. So, "net" is your bottom line—what's left after *all* the expenses are deducted. Are sales up and increasing without the benefit of cutbacks or sell-offs? Or are they declining? You want to see this number increase from one year to the next.

Earnings per share is net earnings (the previous number) divided by the number of outstanding shares (AR page 35, line 1). To help ascertain the rate of the company's growth, follow the EPS over a period of four quarters (one year) or more. This information can also be readily found in Value Line.

Philip Morris gives us five-year information on its Selected Financial Data page (page 33 of the AR). Find the line that says "Basic EPS" and notice that in 1998, earnings (the line just above EPS) and EPS dipped, only to increase again in 1999. If you want to figure out the average growth rate, here's what to do: add the year-to-year percentages and divide by the number of years. In our case, though, we will eliminate the year 1998 as an anomaly. For example: the % growth rate between 1996 and 1997 is 1.5% (2.61 ÷ 2.57 = 1.01556). The number "1" before the decimal simply indicates to us that this is a positive number and can be eliminated in the final result. If there is a zero in front of the decimal, we have a negative number (as seen when calculating the percentage between 1998 and 1997). Continue the percentages, skipping 1998, add the three percentages (1.5% + 22.9% + 17.4%) and divide by 3 to get the average annual rate of growth in EPS (13.9%).

EPS is the amount you might receive if the company paid out *all* their money to its investors. But, that would leave nothing for the company to reinvest in its future. So, the company retains part of the earnings and invests it to make more money. That's why the Percent Return on Equity (ROE) is an important number to ascertain to find out if the company is doing a good job of investing its money—that is, if the company is profitable. This number is also available in Value Line as "return on shr. eq."

The Balance Sheet

Here we are introduced to assets and liabilities. There are three key concerns: assets, liabilities, and shareholders' equity. Assets should equal liabilities plus shareholders' equity. And both assets and liabilities come in two flavors: current (short term) and noncurrent (long term).

1. *Assets*, always shown first in this chart, are what the company owns, like cash, investments, inventories, equipment, buildings,

goodwill, and so on. *Current assets* are what the company can turn into cash within a year, such as treasury bills and certificates of deposit. *Noncurrent assets* are those items that the company does not intend to convert into cash, but can. These assets, for example, real estate and equipment, may take longer than a year to convert into cash.

2. *Liabilities* are debts: what the company owes to banks, for taxes, from accounts payable to suppliers, and any rents and leases. Liabilities are categorized as current (due within a year) or noncurrent (due after a year). When a company's liabilities begin to get out of hand, that's when we may see increased debt or even bankruptcy. One thing to note: If a company doesn't offer a running total for liabilities on the Balance Sheet, as happens with the Coca-Cola Company 2000 annual report, you will have to add everything above the Shareowners' Equity line to get "total" liabilities.

3. *Stockholders'* or *Shareholders' Equity* is essentially part of the company's debt. It is the stockholders' ownership in the company and consists of any new investments plus retained earnings (what's left over after dividends are paid) minus any losses. One number you will see on the Balance Sheet that you do not see on the Equity Sheet (page 38 of the Philip Morris AR) is the par value per share of the common stock. *Par value* is the amount of money the investor would receive for each share held if the stock were liquidated by bankruptcy. If Philip Morris were to close its doors, the stockholders would receive $.33 1/3 per share. Johnson & Johnson would offer $1.00 par value for calling it quits. The total amount that would be owed (par value times number of common shares) is seen under the Common Stock column on the Equity sheet.

What is interesting to note is that Philip Morris has been repurchasing stock over the past several years, thus reducing some of its liability. When you add what the company has retained to reinvest in the business, deduct losses for currency translation, stock repurchases (if any), and any stock held in treasury, you obtain total stockholders' equity.

$$Equity = Assets - Liabilities$$

In the end, both sides of the equation must balance.

Here are a few ratios to use to examine the company's financial position:

Current Ratio

A company's current assets should outweigh its liabilities. There should be more easily liquidated assets to cover any immediate debts. The ratio of assets to liabilities should be greater than 1-to-1. 1.5-to-1 is the more acceptable norm. When the ratio is very high, look for information about a lot of cash on hand and why. Are they accumulating cash for an acquisition? Or are they not putting their cash to its best use? If the ratio is under 1, there may be a sign of excess liabilities that might lead to problems covering any immediate debts or working capital.

$$\text{Current Ratio} = \text{Current Assets} \div \text{Current Liabilities}$$

Let's look at Johnson & Johnson: $15,450 (total current assets) ÷ $7,140 (total current liabilities) = 2.1 to 1.

How about Coca-Cola: $6,620 ÷ $9,321 = .7 (below 1) to 1.

And Philip Morris: $17,238 ÷ $25,949 = .66 (below 1) to 1.

Look for analyses or explanations of excess liabilities for Philip Morris and Coca-Cola.

Quick Ratio

To find out if a company has enough cash-on-hand to pay its debts without using its inventory, we use this ratio to determine quickly available cash.

$$\text{Quick Ratio} = \text{Assets} - \text{Inventory} \div \text{Current Liabilities}$$

Sometimes, a company's inventory can't be turned into cash as quickly as needed, so we use the Quick Ratio, which eliminates the inventory question.

JNJ: $15,450 - $2,842 ÷ $7,140 = 1.76 to 1

This looks healthy—enough cash to pay any immediate debt.

Coca-Cola (KO): $6,620 – $1,066 ÷ $9,321 = .6 to 1

At about the same figure as the current ratio, this tells us there isn't much inventory on hand to turn into quick cash, but that may be the case in food businesses.

Philip Morris: $17,238 – $8,769 ÷ $25,949 = .33 to 1

Half of their current assets are in inventory and their current debt is high (see current portion of long-term debt and settlement charges).

Statement of Cash Flows

Money in. Money out. Where it comes from and where it's going. We all know what this is like. Similar to the income statement, the statement of cash flows tells us how much actual cash the company has made. There are three "net" amounts provided in this statement:

- *operating the business*—net cash made by (+) or used in (–) operating activities. This most important figure tells us whether the company is making money.

- *investing*—net cash made (+) or used (–) in investing activities. These cash investments include property, renovations, overhauling equipment and machinery. Remember that if any of these assets are sold, they provide cash to the bottom line.

- *financing*—net cash made (+) or used (–) by financing activities. Here are some of the ways the company raises cash: selling stocks, borrowing from the bank, or using its cash to buy back stock, paying dividends, or repaying cash loans.

Other items mentioned on the chart are: cash and cash equivalents, acquisitions, and effect of exchange rate changes (which affects every company doing business internationally). These last entries either add to or decrease the preceding subtotals. The result is your net figure on which earnings per share and dividends are based.

Cash helps to pay bills, so it may be helpful to determine the company's *cash flow to assets ratio*. This tells us how much cash the company can generate as compared to its size, but it is important to compare this number with previous years to make sure cash flow isn't on the decline.

Cash from Operations (Statement of Cash Flows) ÷
Total Assets (Balance Sheet) =

Philip Morris 2000: $11,044 ÷ $79,067 = 0.139
or about 14%

Philip Morris 1999: $11,375 ÷ $61,381 = 0.185
or nearly 19%

Philip Morris 1998 $ 8,120 ÷ $59,920 = 0.135
again nearly 14%

This ratio tells us that cash flow is staying at a reasonable rate. Make sure when you examine cash flow that it never dips below 10% or is on a decline.

Statements of Stockholders' Equity

The information on this page can also be seen in a reduced version on the balance sheet under the liabilities column. Stockholders' or shareholders' equity, as we mentioned earlier, is the difference between total assets and total liabilities. The *par value* total figure we saw on the balance sheet is the number we see under the Common Stock column or $935.

From the yearly total earnings, a certain amount is retained by the company and reinvested into the growth of the company. The number you see at the bottom of the column for "retained earnings" or "earnings reinvested" is a cumulative number. Each year, net earnings minus declared dividends and stock options are added to the previous balance, giving the "retained" earnings amount. The company wants to make money by investing these retained earnings and they want the return to be good. To find out what the company earns when it invests the shareholders' money, use the *return on equity ratio* (ROE, called % Earned Net Worth in Value Line).

Net Earnings After Taxes or Net Income (S of E, S of CF) ÷
Shareholders' Equity =

Here is the Philip Morris example:

$8,510 ÷ $33,481 = .254 or 25.4% return on equity

Twenty-five percent is a very good rate of return on an investment. For the investor this is yet another way to determine if management is running the company profitably. High returns create higher assets for the company and are usually indicative of companies that pay their shareholders well.

We are provided with three years of information on the Equity page and can calculate the year-to-year results. These numbers should remain stable or continue to increase to reflect good money management. If the numbers are in decline (by whole point movement and not just small fractions), it should send up a red flag. A little research or a call to Investor Relations can help determine why there is a decline in the rate of return.

The second ratio that is important to understand is *debt to equity*. In other words, when financing the company's assets, what proportion of shareholders' equity is used as compared to loans? We use long-term debt in this ratio (although some like to use total liabilities) because it gives a clearer picture of monies used from loans as opposed to the combination of total liabilities that includes long-term and short-term debt, dividends, taxes, and items such as health care costs, and so on.

Long Term Debt (Balance Sheets) ÷ Equity (Statement of Equity) =

Guidelines: A figure below one means that financing is coming mostly from equity—money provided by shareholders. A number above one means that assets are financed mainly with debt or loans. This could put the company in a precarious position if interest rates are high or if the company is in need of additional financing.

TABLE 5.1   Ratio Summary Table

Name of Ratio	Explanation	Ratio	What to Look For
Current	Comparing current assets to liabilities— looking for cash on hand	Total current assets ÷ current liabilities = Current Ratio	> 1 to 1
Quick	Comparing assets to liabilities without using inventory	Assets – inventory ÷ current liabilities = Quick Ratio	> 1 to 1
Cash Flow to Assets	Available cash	Cash from operations ÷ total assets = Cash Flow	> 10%
Return on Equity (ROE)	Return on investments	Net earnings ÷ shareholder equity = % return	> 15%
Debt to Equity	What portion of shareholders' equity is used to finance assets	Long-term debt ÷ equity = ratio	> 1.00 and < 2.00
Debt	How much debt the company has	Long-term debt ÷ (long-term debt + shareholders' equity) = %	< .33 or 33%

Example: Philip Morris's debt/equity ratio:

$$\$18{,}255 \div \$15{,}005 = 1.22$$

This calculation tells us that Philip Morris is relying more on loan money to finance its capital structure and not dipping so heavily into the shareholders' equity. This ratio is certainly within the realm of reasonableness. And, remember that Philip Morris is using equity to buy back stock. This will keep their ratio in check. When we see a debt-to-equity ratio reaching 2, we can look for heavy debt and potential problems.

Before we leave the financials, there is one last ratio concerning capital structure or the long-term financing of the company through common and preferred stock, long-term debt and equity, that may be helpful to understand. This is the *debt ratio*. Debt is one of those inevitable factors of doing business. But we also want to make sure that a company isn't carrying too much debt, perhaps no more than 33 percent.

Long-term Debt ÷ (Long-term Debt + Shareholders' Equity) =

Philip Morris Example:

$18,255 ÷ ($18,255 + $15,005) = $18,255 ÷ $33,260 or .55

Half of the company's capitalization is from debt.

Guidelines: Compare this with what other companies in this industry show as a debt ratio to see if this is high or par for the course.

The Notes to the Financial Statements

Don't skip the footnotes or Notes to the Financial Statements. Whatever is going on with a company that affects its bottom line—its ability to make a profit, and pay debts or dividends—will be explained in the notes. Any acquisitions, divestitures, pension and benefit plans, lawsuits, or anything else regarding money—where it comes from, how it's used, and where it's going—is addressed here.

CHAPTER SIX

The Economy and the Stock Market

KEY TERMS

- Consumer Price Index (CPI)
  An inflationary indicator, published monthly, that measures the change in the cost of a fixed group of products and services.

- economic indicators
  Statistics gathered on a regular basis that indicate how the economy is doing.

- Gross Domestic Product (GDP)
  The total market value of all final goods and services produced in a country in a given year.

- Producer Price Index (PPI)
  An inflationary indicator published by the U.S. Bureau of Labor Statistics to evaluate wholesale price levels in the economy.

- yield curve
  The difference between long interest rates and short interest rates, and an indicator of general economic conditions.

THE CYCLE OF MONEY

Just about everything we do has an impact on the economy and it all boils down to the flow of money. When we make money and spend money the government has a way of tracking its flow and determining what it means to the health of our economy. Let's look at the flow of money.

- You have a job and receive a paycheck for work you do in helping to manufacture or sell a product. That product is shipped and sold at regular intervals, for which your company gets paid and, in turn, pays you.

- You use your paycheck to pay your bills, buy essentials and nonessentials, all of which are products and services provided by someone else—the mortgage company, the grocery store, and the movie theater.

- These companies accumulate money to help continue their businesses and to pay their workers, who then use their paychecks to pay bills and buy consumer goods.

Here's an example: You buy a can of corn at the supermarket. Someone had to grow the corn, harvest the corn, process the corn, ship it to the supermarket, place it on the shelf, check you out and take your money. In buying that can of corn, you have just supported several industries and the people who work in them, including your father-in-law, who works for the corn-canning company.

Your father-in-law just bought you an anniversary gift—you're going to Disneyland where your daughter works. His gift has just supported the airlines and his granddaughter, so to speak. She then uses her salary to buy a car from the very same company for which you work. You now see how the money cycle works. Like pebbles plunked into a pool, rings are created that keep moving, overlapping, and spreading in all directions. Each one affects the next: this is how money "flows." When you understand what each of these water rings or cycles represents as a factor affecting the economy, you can begin to see trends, or movement, in the economy that ultimately affect the stock market.

ECONOMIC INDICATORS

These factors, or *Economic Indicators*, are statistical groupings of information gathered and presented by the federal government or private research firms to show general trends in the economy. These statistics are compiled into indexes that are categorized by economists into three types: leading, lagging, and coincident. Together, these three indexes make up the *Leading Economic Indicator* or LEI. A *leading indicator* (there are 10 in the index) is a forward-looking or future indicator. It detects and predicts future economic trends. A *coincident indicator* (there are 4 in the index) varies in tune with the economy. It is directly related to the current state of the economy. A *lagging indicator* (there are 7 in the index) generally rises or falls after a change in the current economy has occurred or a change in the coincident index has taken place. Essentially, a lagging indicator reflects what has already happened.

Generally released on a monthly basis, these indicators or the LEI, in a cumulative measure, give us an overview of recent economic trends, the current state of our economy, and a projection of where the economy is going. When we hear about the state of the economy, it is referred to in one of its four phases: expansion (time of growth), peak, recession (defined by at least two straight quarters of contraction in the economy as reported by the Gross Domestic Product), and trough (reaching bottom). When we look back over the last several years, we can recall hearing or reading about expansion (1999), peak (2000), and even recession (2001).

The components of the three indexes—leading, coincident and lagging—that make up the LEI are as follows:

Leading Index—where the economy is going

1. Average hours worked per week for manufacturing workers. The employment situation.
2. Initial jobless claims—Average weekly initial state unemployment insurance claims.
3. New factory orders—Manufacturers' new orders for consumer goods and materials.
4. Vendor performance—Purchasing Managers Index.
5. Manufacturers' new orders for non-military capital goods.
6. Housing starts and new building permits.

7. Stock prices (S&P 500).

8. Money supply, M2—adjusted for inflation.

9. The interest rate spread between 10-year Treasury bonds and federal funds rate.

10. Consumer confidence.

Coincident Index—the economy's status now

1. Employees on non-agricultural payrolls.

2. Personal income.

3. Industrial production.

4. Manufacturing and trade sales.

Lagging Index—where the economy has been

1. Average duration of employment.

2. Inventories to sales ratio, manufacturing and trade.

3. Labor cost per unit of output, manufacturing.

4. Average prime rate.

5. Commercial and industrial loans.

6. Consumer installment credit to personal income ratio.

7. Consumer price index (CPI) for services.

We will concentrate on the ten leading indicators, with some explanation of the other indicators where applicable, since the leading indicators are considered to offer a glimpse some six to nine months into the future. Knowing what to look for in the future of the economy will help us make better decisions about our investments.

1. The Employment Situation (from The Employment Report)

The Labor Department, or the Bureau of Labor and Statistics, takes a monthly measure of 250 regions and every major industry and reports several key factors: the number of new jobs created, the unemployment rate, average hourly wages earned, and the length of the average work-week for manufacturing workers. Generally, we hear only about the unemployment rate on the news; but taken together this data gives us an overall picture of whether the labor market is increasing or decreasing, which directly affects manufacturing and inflation, and can move the stock market accordingly.

Because of the timely nature of this report (it reaches us within a week), it is considered one of the top indicators of the health of our economy and, depending on whether it's a positive or negative report, can signal what to expect from some of the other indicators, like Retail Sales. The indicator specific to the average hours worked per week is important because it tends to lead the business cycle, causing manufacturers to adjust work hours before increasing or decreasing their workforce.

Each of the components of the Employment Situation influences other indicators.

Indicator	*What it affects*
Average hourly wage	personal income
	wages and salaries component of Employment Cost Index
Manufacturing hours	industrial production
Change in construction jobs—housing starts	construction spending

2. Initial Jobless Claims

The Labor Department reports weekly (every Thursday) on the number of people filing for state unemployment insurance claims for the first time or making new claims. Though also considered timely and a good gauge of the labor market, a trend in the labor market generally takes four weeks to unveil itself. When unemployment conditions worsen, as we saw with many of the technology layoffs, and no new jobs are created, we hear that "initial claims have risen." Again, this is considered a leading indicator in the business cycle and occasionally this report will move the market.

Indicator	*What it affects*
Employment index	manufacturing employment

3. New Factory Orders—Manufacturers' New Orders for Consumer Goods and Materials (Factory Report by the Census Bureau)

Also referred to as the Preliminary Report on Manufacturers' Shipments, Inventories and Orders, this monthly report tells us about overall sales including orders that have been shipped, goods that are sitting in inventory, and orders placed that are as yet unfilled or in the process of being manufactured. Because this news is two months old, the stock market rarely reacts to it. However, it is important to note inventory levels (see Chapter 5, The Financials) when analyzing a company's annual report because an abundance of goods sitting in a warehouse, as we have seen with the personal computer (PC) market, usually signals a slowdown in retail sales, which, in turn, affects new orders placed and manufacturing. On the flip side, an abundance of inventory does tend to reduce prices to the consumer, helping to move inventory.

Indicator	*What it affects*
New Orders index	factory orders

4. Vendor Performance

Taken from the Purchasing Managers Index (PMI), which covers new orders, inventory levels, productions, supplier deliveries, and the employment environment, the monthly Vendor Performance portion of the index reports on how quickly manufacturers are receiving their goods from suppliers. Initially, any sign of slow deliveries from vendors creates an increase in demand from manufacturers for their supplies, but a series of slowdowns can create a stall in manufacturing and lessen the ability of manufacturers to fulfill orders.

This index is reported in percentage change and shows an increase, decrease, or status quo from one month to the next. The numbers indicate the following:

- A PMI result over 50% indicates an expansion in manufacturing.
- A PMI result under 50% means that manufacturing is on the decline.

The PMI report is timely and extremely important to the financial markets. Investors pay close attention to this report because, along with the Consumer Price Index (CPI), it can detect the possibility of inflation. Supplier deliveries is a key component of the Leading Economic Indicators (LEI) and because it is such crucial information, a change in the PMI can move the market and can predict manufacturing activity in the months to come.

Indicator	*What it affects*
Production index	industrial production
Prices index	Production Price Index
New orders index	factory orders

We have mentioned the Consumer Price Index several times and though it is not one of the ten leading indicators, it is one of the most closely followed economic indicators from the Bureau of Labor and Statistics. The CPI reports thousands of prices on consumer goods (like clothing and toilet paper) and services (like medical care and education). When you spend money on goods and services, the government knows how much you pay. This helps the government determine how effective its economic policy has been and is an important indicator of inflation, or the rate at which those prices are rising. Remember, if the cost of goods goes up, our purchasing ability (the value of each dollar we spend) goes down. So, when gasoline costs $1.00 per gallon and goes up to $2.00 per gallon, we are only getting half as much for our money (in this case, ½ gallon for every dollar spent). This leads us back to the Federal Reserve Board (The Fed), which checks the rate of inflation by increasing short-term interest rates and stimulates spending by decreasing those rates. Increasing rates can affect the financial markets negatively. Decreasing rates can affect the market positively. When we hear about the CPI, the term "core rate" or "core" means that the more volatile energy and food prices are excluded from the reporting to provide a better inflationary picture.

Indicator	*What it affects*
CPI for medical care	employment cost index
CPI for gasoline	retail sales report
CPI for vehicles	personal income & consumption report

5. Manufacturers' new orders for non-military capital goods

Like manufacturers' orders for consumer goods and materials, this report includes final shipments (sales) and unfilled orders (inventory and manufacturing), only this report eliminates any goods for defense purposes. It is stipulated in percentage changes on a monthly basis but also offers annual comparisons to show overall increases or decreases in orders for durable goods (longer-lasting items such as cars and appliances), which comprise 57% of the new order results.

Indicator	*What it affects*
PMI	Production Price Index (PPI)

Formerly known as the "Wholesale Price Index," the PPI reports the cost of goods before it hits the retailer. Though not as strong an indicator as the Consumer Price Index, it portends the CPI, which can tell us about the rate of inflation. Like the CPI, the "core rate" of the PPI also excludes the volatile sectors of food and energy.

Indicator	*What it affects*
PPI	CPI
	reflects industrial production

6. Housing Starts and New Building Permits

The Census Bureau gives a monthly accounting of how many residential housing units are being built and how many building permits have been issued. Residential housing is mostly single-family homes, but the Housing Starts Report includes apartment-house units. When people build houses, it is considered an indication that the economy is healthy.

Indicator	*What it affects*
Housing starts	residential investment portion of the Gross Domestic Product (GDP)
	construction activity
	employment
	other economic production

Referred to as the "Nation's Report Card" of economic health, the GDP is considered highly significant to the financial market. Reported on a quarterly basis (last business day of January, April, July, and October), with monthly updates, the GDP represents the dollar value of all domestic goods and services purchased. There are four components to the report:

- Consumption—56%[1] of the GDP including durable goods, non-durable goods, and services.
- Investment Spending—14% of the GDP including non-residential (factories and equipment), residential (housing), and change in business inventories.
- Government Spending—14% of the GDP including defense, roads, schools.
- Trade Balance (or Net Exports)—13% of the GDP, which includes exports minus imports (notice the negative net amount for the past several years due to more imports than exports).

Indicator	*What it affects*
GDP	interest rates
	inflation
	stock and bond rates

---

[1]GDP component percentages are based on GDP information of April 27, 2000.

COMPARE THESE TWO EXCERPTS from CNNfn regarding the GDP quarterly report:

"The U.S. economy finished 1999 with its strongest growth rate of the year while labor costs and prices crept higher, the government reported Friday—signs that record levels of employment and resilient consumer spending may be starting to ignite inflation.

Gross domestic product grew at a 5.8 percent annual rate in the fourth quarter, above the 5.5 percent increase expected and the 5.7 percent rate recorded in the third quarter."   —January 28, 2000

"The U.S. economy grew at the slowest rate in more than eight years in the second quarter as businesses slashed spending, the government said Friday, the latest signs of malaise in the world's largest economy. . . . Gross domestic product (GDP)—the broadest measure of the nation's economy—grew at a 0.7 percent annual rate in the quarter . . . compared with a revised 1.3 percent growth in the first quarter and a revised 5.7 percent rate a year earlier. . . . It was the weakest since the economy shrank 0.1 percent in the first quarter of 1993."   —July 27, 2000

7. The Standard & Poor's 500

As we have seen in Chapter 2, the S&P 500 Index, which reflects about 80% of the total stock market capitalization, is a movement indicator. Increases or decreases in the S&P 500 reflect the general mood of investors and interest rate movements.

Indicator	What it affects
S&P 500	reflects interest rates
	future economic activity

8. Money Supply—M2

Money supply, or how much money is in circulation, is measured as M1, M2, and M3.

M1 = Currency in circulation and in checking accounts.

M2 = M1 plus savings accounts, time deposits (CDs) under $100,000, retail money market funds, and overnight purchase agreements.

M3 = M2 plus time deposits (CDs) over $100,000, institutional money market funds (like your 401k), and term repurchasing agreements.

The government, or the Fed (Federal Reserve Board), regulates the supply of money by placing an annual range on the growth of that money supply. For instance, the target range for M2 growth in 1998 and 1999 was 1% to 5%. However, it grew 8.5% in 1998, subsequently falling to 3.4% in 1999. The growth of the money supply is also closely linked to interest rates (Fed Fund Rates). When the Fed cuts interest rates, or the rate at which banks lend to each other, its intention is to spur the economy. Though it may take months before it trickles down to the consumer as lower bank loan interest rates, it is nonetheless done with the idea that more money will eventually flow. When the Fed raises interest rates, they are trying to curb inflation or shorten the money supply.

Before the Federal Reserve Board meets (eight times per year, although only four meetings are mandated), they issue a report called the "Summary of Commentary on Current Economic Conditions by Federal Reserve District," commonly referred to as The Beige Book. Not meant to be a statistical report, the descriptive coverage in The Beige Book reports current economic conditions and gives the status of change in the economy since the last meeting of the Fed. Since it comes from a variety of sources other than the Fed, it does help the Fed decide what to do about interest rates and the money supply.

9. The Interest Rate Spread

This difference between long interest rates (10-year bond) and short interest rates (federal funds rate) is referred to as the "yield curve" or yield and is an indicator of general financial conditions. When the spread is said to fall or is decreased between the two, it means that short rates (federal fund rates) are high. When short rates become higher than long rates (called an inversion), we clearly have an indicator of recession.

$$\text{yield curve} \uparrow = \text{low short rates}$$

$$\text{yield curve} \downarrow = \text{high short rates}$$

10. Consumer Confidence Index (CCI)

Every month the Consumer Confidence Board and the University of Michigan independently collect data from households about how they spend their money. Having money to spend is directly connected to jobs, wages, and lower interest rates, which brings us back to the Fed. If they see an indication that consumer confidence is down—people aren't spending money on consumer goods or building or buying new homes, and so on—guess what happens? They cut the interest rates. But, the effect of these rate changes takes six to eight months to trickle down to the consumer level, and generally it only takes three to six months to get an indication of consumer confidence. While a positive CCI report may temporarily boost the market, the three to six month "moving average" trend is far more significant to the economy and the stock market.

Indicator	*What it affects*
New jobs	consumer confidence
Consumer confidence	interest rates
Interest rates	stock prices

THE LOWERING of interest rates often affects the stock market positively. Since 1954, The Federal Reserve Board has cut interest rates to help stimulate the economy 14 times. Within twelve months, in all but one case, the S&P increased.

When we see stock prices rise and fall with news of the economy, we now know why it happens and how to interpret it. Those companies with sound business practices, and that have managed to remain flexible and responsive through economic downturns—like the giants—are companies that will continue in the forefront.

A CENTURY OF
INVESTING HISTORY

Seeds of Ideas, Winds of Change— The Second Industrial Revolution through the Turn of the Century

A giant "anything," by the nature of its size, may be powerful but tends to be slower moving. Think of the giant tortoise, the giant Panda, or any other giant species. This is true for stocks as well.

Many of the giant, "old economy" companies around today started in the 19th and 20th centuries: Procter & Gamble, IBM, Philip Morris, Johnson & Johnson, Coca-Cola, General Motors, American Express, McDonald's and Wal-Mart, and a host of other "household names." When we think of giant stocks or giant companies such as the ten we have listed, we might think this means there is no room for growth; but the ability to achieve and maintain their status comes through innovation, flexibility, and marketing. Without new ideas, research and marketing, and a willingness to reinvent themselves from time to time, many would have gone the way of the dinosaurs or dotcoms. Take Coca-Cola, for example. Here is a company with essentially one product, yet they have remained the number one soft drink manufacturer in the world. How did they do that? Foresight. Growth through expansion and acquisition. Change through research and innovation. These elements underscore how all ten of these giants have not only endured but stand powerfully within the new millennium.

Coca-Cola made its debut in 1886. Originally conceived by pharmacist John Pemberton as a medicinal drink, Coca-Cola as we know it today was the second of his formulations based on coca leaves and kola nuts. This backyard-concocted, caramel-colored drink became a fad after making its way to the soda fountain at Jacob's Pharmacy in Atlanta where it was test-marketed at 5 cents a glass. In 1887, Pemberton's health began to decline so he sold off two-thirds of his company: one third each to Willis Venable and George Lowndes who, in turn, sold their portions to Woolfolk Walker and his sister Margaret Dozier. Interestingly, Venable also gave his share to Joseph Jacobs of Jacob's Pharmacy. To keep his idea alive, Pemberton, who still owned one-third of the company, ran an ad in 1887 looking for investors and received $2,000 each from three men: Mayfield, Murphey, and Bloodworth. So, now there were several people involved in the manufacture of Coca-Cola, whose name was actually conceived by Pemberton's bookkeeper Frank Robinson, as was the cursive logo design we see today. Jacobs, incidentally, was the one who added carbonation from the soda fountain. By May 1886, they placed their first advertisement in the Atlanta Journal—on the patent medicine page.

With Pemberton's health failing, Robinson seems to have been the only one who kept the faith against the looming threat of losing the business. In June 1887, the cursive Coca-Cola trademark was patented and by year's end, seeing great potential, Asa Candler, a businessman and entrepreneur who firmly believed in the power of marketing, advertising and promotion, entered the picture. Two weeks after Pemberton's death on August 16, 1888, Asa Candler bought out the remaining interest from Dozier and Walker for what some reports say was $1,000 for the rights to the formula, and by 1891 became sole proprietor of what he would incorporate as "The Coca-Cola Company."

Candler's keen sensibility in getting the word out—through advertising, complimentary drinks, display posters and trinkets, and even the precursor to the billboard—created consumer desire and made it possible to distribute the product even more widely. With the Industrial Revolution came bottling technology in 1894, and by 1895, Asa Candler proclaimed, "Coca-Cola is now drunk in every State and territory in the U.S." By 1898, Coca-Cola entered the Mexican and Canadian markets, and by the turn of the century Candler granted rights to the bottling of Coca-Cola, laying the company's foundation for further expansion and success.

FRANK ROBINSON, Pemberton's bookkeeper, named the soft drink product Coca-Cola and created the script logo with the two swash *C*'s that he thought would look good in advertising.

Had it not been for the Industrial Revolution and the advent of mechanization, perhaps Coca-Cola would not have become so entrenched in our lifestyle as it is today. By 1851, the Industrial Revolution had taken its hold on the United States. Though the Industrial Revolution began over a half century earlier in Europe when the U.S. was still in its infancy and still an agriculturally based society, America would soon catch up and surpass the rest of the industrial world.

The 1851 World's Fair at London's Crystal Palace paved the way for vigorous growth and placed the United States first in manufacturing by the end of the century. The United States advanced on the new industrial world, ringing in a Second Industrial Revolution with advantages only the young nation could have had: new lands to be explored, a willingness by the people to grow economically, and a self-sufficient nation with the ability to move goods, people, ideas, and capital across the continent. One of the first important advances allowing for American growth was in communications; the simple Morse telegraph (1837) that required relay signals every twenty miles was soon replaced by duplex telegraphy—the means of sending several messages over a single wire; and by 1874, Thomas Edison invented quadruplex telegraphy whereby two messages could be sent in either direction simultaneously. Fueling this internal growth was transportation. By 1860, half the world's railroad tracks were in the U.S. Roads were laid and canals were built.

European and British inventors, entrepreneurs, and wealth seek-
ers flooded into America; yet even with this influx there was a short-
age of labor, so American industrialists turned to the development of
machinery to replace human labor. Special-purpose machinery was
developed for mass production of parts that could be assembled into
finished products. This "American system of production," or mass
production, created products more uniform than their handcrafted
counterparts. Originally seen in New England in products such as
clocks and locks, it also became the system for the mass production
of firearms by Colt, reapers by McCormick, and sewing machines
by Singer.

The American Civil War took its toll on labor forces but also
helped bring about some important innovations. During the war, the
many casualties who required surgery and care in the fields died from
inadequate sterilization procedures, something left over from the European tradition of reusing equipment. Other problems included
workers operating bare-handed and in blood-spattered dusters worn
over street clothes, along with packing wounds with cotton floor-
sweepings from the textile mills. It wasn't until 1876 that a young
pharmacist, Robert Wood Johnson, heard a speech about diminishing
germs in the operating room by the prominent English surgeon,
Joseph Lister. Lister applied Louis Pasteur's information on bacteria
and infection; Johnson embraced the idea of sterilization and created
a new type of surgical dressing, individually wrapped and accessible
for use without further risk of contamination. Johnson had already
formed a partnership in 1874 to produce bandages using India rubber;
but in 1885, he enlisted his two brothers, Edward Mead Johnson and
James Wood Johnson, to enter the surgical dressings industry. Johnson
& Johnson was born. Extensively promoting antiseptic surgical procedures, they even published a book entitled "Modern Methods of Antiseptic Wound Treatment." Continuing their devotion to these
standards, the brothers, along with noted scientific writer Fred Kilmer
(father of World War I poet-hero Joyce Kilmer) established a bacterio-
logical laboratory to successfully employ technology to ensure aseptic
conditions for creating a sterile product. By 1897, using the same
method, they improved the technique for sterilizing catgut sutures
for operations.

CATGUT IS A PRODUCT used as far back as Egyptian times, though it received its name from the medieval musical instrument *kit*, which used the intestinal material from sheep and bovine. It was unlikely that cats were ever employed for this purpose. Uses for catgut, other than sutures: musical instruments, tennis rackets, and archery bows.

The Second Industrial Revolution in America was a time for many firsts: the telegraph, telephone, light bulb, diesel engine, and Marconi wireless, to name a few. With each came a multitude of changes and advances and with these changes came a shift in American society. Rural life declined. Urban life expanded with each new industry. In 1860, there were only nine American cities with a population of 100,000 or more: by 1900, there were 38. The American workforce increasingly turned its collective face toward industry and away from farm work. From the 1790 census to 1900, we saw a steady shift in the labor force, with farm workers declining from 75 percent to 40 percent of the workforce. Now came a new set of problems.

The steady immigration and urbanization of people created a need to keep better track of the American populace. Old methods of calculation would be endless and inefficient, so in 1890 the U.S. Census Bureau ran a contest to help create a better method of tabulation. The winner of this contest was Herman Hollerith, a German immigrant and Census Bureau statistician. He devised a machine that used electrical current that sensed the holes in the census punch cards and kept a running total of the data. Sound anything like the voting machines used in some places today? This success led to the creation of the Tabulating Machine Company in 1896. With continuing growth into the next century—growth that would include the merger of several companies; marketing new products ranging from commercial scales, industrial time recorders, meat and cheese slicers, all the way to tabulators and punch cards; the overseeing of international expansion; generous sales incentives for employees and perks for their families—this company would come to be known to us as International Business Machines, or IBM.

Industrialization, mechanization, need, greed, ingenuity—these led to newer, bigger, better products for life and leisure: Frederic Miller's bottled beer, Pemberton's Coca-Cola, fine cigars by Englishman Philip Morris, Emanuele Ronzoni's macaroni, C.W. Post's cereal Grape-Nuts, Jell-O brand gelatin desserts, P.J. Towle's blended table syrup, processed meats by Oscar Mayer, Entenmann's home-delivered baked goods, and soap from Procter & Gamble, to name only a few. Many products we think of as new today have been with us for generations. Companies and entire industries have grown and thrived around the marketing and branding of products and services to each new generation that has come along. The "giants" have discovered the secrets of keeping business not only alive, but well, into the next century and beyond.

Procter & Gamble is a case of 99 44/100% pure happenstance. Like so many others, William Procter came from England to seek his fortune in the American west. He got only as far as Cincinnati when his wife became ill and died. He never moved on, but instead settled there and became a candle maker. James Gamble came from Ireland to seek his fortune and remained in Cincinnati for medical attention himself. He stayed and became an apprentice soap maker.

The two men met when they courted and married the two Norris sisters, Olivia and Elizabeth, and united their businesses at the suggestion of their father-in-law. In 1837 Procter & Gamble was born. Though national difficulties made this an inauspicious time to start a business—and there were fourteen other similar businesses in Cincinnati—the records at P&G indicate that the two men made and sold their products together beginning in April of that year, formalized their agreement in August with a pledge of $3,596.47 apiece, and signed an agreement in October. Either a Procter or a Gamble headed up the company until 1930 when William Cooper Procter, grandson of co-founder William Procter, retired. During their reign, the company created some of the most innovative consumer products to have withstood the test of time. They also created branding and trademarks.

The P&G trademark of the Moon and Stars was a symbol originally used by the company in the 1850s to distinguish cases of Star Candles from boxes of soap products. This simple, elegant mark became associated with P&G and was officially adopted and used on all P&G products and stationery by the 1860s.

Gamble's son, James Norris Gamble, a chemist by education, created the company's oldest name-brand product, Ivory Soap, in 1879. Procter's son, Harley, named the soap after reading the Biblical passage "out of ivory palaces." By 1882, the company allocated $11,000 to a national advertising campaign of this brand.

But P&G was not only an innovator of products, it was also a pioneer in employee relationships. In 1887, William Cooper Procter, the founder's grandson, recognizing that employees who owned a piece of the company worked harder and were more loyal, instituted a voluntary profit-sharing program.

P&G's innovation in product marketing and branding continued into the next century with plant expansions throughout the United States and Canada. Urbanization and sheer will created the company; research helped keep it abreast of consumer needs.

THE CENTURY TURNS

It is often said that more progress has been made in our lifetime than at any other time in history. But the Second Industrial Revolution, which takes us into the twentieth century, saw an equal amount of change.

Massive immigration continued, but now it was paralleled by a growing concern that reared its head in the name of nationalism. Exclusionary acts were issued that fueled racist feelings even though the growing immigrant population helped form the country politically, socially, and economically. And it is documented that at the turn of the century, this very same population helped boost the tobacco industry to one of the top three industries in America, along with steel and oil.

This was certainly not a new industry, given that the tobacco plant can be tracked as far back as 6000 B.C. and the use of tobacco appears throughout all documented history. But it has always been an industry surrounded by controversy: America's oldest tobacco manufacturing company, P. Lorrilard (1760) coincides with the first clinical studies and warnings about the effects of tobacco, in this case snuff, on one's health (1761). Though fuel for controversy, throughout the 18th century tobacco was used as monetary exchange; it even helped finance the American Revolution. By the end of the 1700s, the U.S.

Congress decided to help itself to some of tobacco's prosperity by is-
suing a tax on snuff. Again, in 1862, the government issued its first
U.S. federal tax on tobacco to help pay for the Civil War, some $3 mil-
lion. From the very beginning, government and tobacco would hold
hands and alternatively do combat.

The U.S. struggled through its first anti-tobacco movement beginning in 1836 against the explosive tobacco industry with the mechanization of cigarette manufacturing by 1860 and the first marketing
strategy employed by P. Lorillard: to celebrate the 100th Anniversary
of the firm, the Lorillard Company randomly inserted $100 bills into
celebratory packs of cigarettes.

In 1890, the government listed tobacco as a drug, only to drop it
from the list in 1906 to ensure the passage of the Food and Drug Act.
The turn of the century also saw various states ban the selling or smoking of tobacco. Though the anti-cigarette movement did close down
many small concerns, 1900 also saw an all-time high sale of 4.4 billion
cigarettes.

America's prosperity and growth was always a good news/bad
news situation: The Food and Drug Act was an important advancement in the safety regulation and honest labeling of foods to protect
the public; environmental laws were also enacted; Victorianism was
dead and buried; moving pictures were the new "new thing," with
Thomas Edison's commercially successful *The Great Train Robbery*;
mass production reduced the prices of goods, making the Sears, Roe-
buck and Montgomery Ward catalogs bestsellers; the Wright Brothers
made their first flight at Kitty Hawk; and, finally, the automobile
closed the transportation gap.

What would come to be known as General Motors began in 1897
as the Olds Motor Company and by 1901 was the first American car to
be manufactured in quantity. Other notable dates include:

- 1900—there are 96 auto deaths and some 8,000 cars on the
  road.
- 1902—Cadillac Automobile Company is formed.
- 1903—Buick Motor Company is incorporated.
- 1903—Henry Ford introduces the Model A at an affordable
  price of $700 to $900.

- 1906—Buick builds its first 4-cylinder car, a 1907 Model D.

- 1907—Ford announces his goal to make a less expensive car. The answer: the Model T.

- 1908—General Motors Company is formed by William Durant, who brought together Buick and Olds.

- 1909—GM purchases Cadillac for $5.5 million and buys a half interest in Oakland Motor Car Co. (Pontiac).

- 1913—Ford introduces the assembly line and now produces half of the cars on the road.

A boon to the automotive industry, Ford's assembly line was inspired by Chicago's meat-packing plants, but Ford took it one step further by hiring a time management consultant to create the exact number of steps and range of motion that workers should use.

America's pace was picking up. Motoring became a national pastime, topped by "the Sunday drive." Speed became an elixir, so limits were deemed necessary to protect the public. The first state to place a limit on speed was Connecticut. Around 1900 it mandated speed limits of 12 miles per hour in rural areas and 8 mph in the cities. By 1906, fifteen states had instituted speed limits of 20 mph.

Nothing would stop Americans as they carried on their quest for more, bigger, and better over the next century—not even war.

CHAPTER EIGHT

World War I

Whereas the Industrial Revolution and the turn of the century brought unprecedented expansion, involvement in World War I blind-sided the American economy. After remaining neutral until 1917, the United States declared war on Germany, subsequently depleting the workforce by putting over four million people in combat. Thrown off-balance and without a previous model for retooling, companies scrambled for a plan that worked. German industrialization was at its peak. Germany's occupation of France provided additional industrial and mineral resources, forcing France to rely on U.S. supplies. Behind in modernization, Britain also relied heavily on U.S. production. Military success was critically dependent on the country's ability to produce a continuous supply of goods for its armed forces.

The giants who rose and reigned during this period were those with "scramble-vision"—companies that saw a need, mobilized, and then delivered.

With labor forces critically low in factories, a northern migration of black workers from the south ensued. Women replaced men in traditional factory jobs. While both groups of workers were crucial to the war effort, they ultimately fared differently: the status of the Black worker had not improved and their new communities faced racial tensions, harassment, and street riots in the North, while the American woman finally realized the passage of the 19th Amendment for women's rights. An encroaching fear of German immigrants and their descendants prompted extreme measures and repressive laws.

Industry rose to the occasion by improving upon the mass production techniques developed during the Second Industrial Revolution. Government stepped in and began to regulate output and product usage, including the railroads, coal, and gasoline so the war effort could be supported. It even urged the voluntary rationing of food by declaring "meatless Mondays" and "wheatless Wednesdays."

The youngest of the industries on the scene, automobile manufacturing, saw enormous growth with the introduction of the assembly line. The oldest of the businesses, tobacco, increased its sales 25% with the continuing wave of immigrants.

The arts flourished during this decade. Art, music, and architecture saw the likes of the realism of the Ash Can School of Painting and futurist Joseph Stella. Georgia O'Keeffe, James Whistler, Mary Cassatt, and Alfred Steiglitz are names we recognize from this era. And Americans began a love affair with Norman Rockwell's representations of American life on the covers of the Saturday Evening Post beginning in 1916. The New York Public Library, Grand Central Station, the Massachusetts Institute of Technology (MIT), and works by Frank Lloyd Wright were all cause for celebration.

Books took top billing with many bestsellers that remain classics today: *The Secret Garden*, *Sons and Lovers*, *Of Human Bondage*, and *Tarzan of the Apes*, to name a few. The war spurred a new classic: the war story. In 1919, the number one bestseller was *Four Horsemen of the Apocalypse*.

The rise of culture, even pop culture, seems antithetical in a society fraught with growth problems and on the verge of war, but the public took their leisure time seriously. Luxuries became as important as necessities, so film, theater, cars, fashion, vacationing, nightlife and all it affected spewed forth. The war would change that, even if only temporarily.

By 1910, the automobile became a common sight. Mass production and demand saw the first luxury cars roll off the line, with Cadillac topping the bill for GM. Not sitting back for long, research and development brought the industry the electric self-starter, a thermostatically controlled cooling system, and the big V-8 engine in 1914. During America's involvement in the war, William Durant, head of General Motors, sustained the company's growth with continued improvements and acquisitions: GM manufactured tractors (ultimately a loss for the company), acquired a major stake in the Fisher Body Company (you've no doubt heard the phrase "Body by Fisher"), offered auto maintenance and servicing, and created the GM Acceptance Corporation to help financing. Durant also had intuition and foresight enough to try his hand at new products. He invested in a developing company that planned to manufacture an electric icebox.

The years prior to entry into WWI were also fraught with problems for GM. Ford made the most durable and affordable car with its Model T, the car for the masses. Financial stresses in 1910 and again in 1916 forced GM into reorganization. GM did, however, manage to expand its manufacturing borders and increase its sales by creating an export division. This decade would set the stage for GM, Ford, and Chrysler to dominate the auto industry and become known forever as the "Big Three."

American Express is a company that saw most of this decade's change that resulted from external pressures. War in the European theater proved profitable for American Express. While continuing its travelers cheques operations, American Express expanded its services to cover the needs of Americans in Europe by providing overseas freight services, financial services, and currency exchange. Once the U.S. became engaged in the war, the government nationalized all railway and delivery services at home by merging the companies and their equipment and employees into one source. This might have put American Express out of business except for their shift in venue to Europe. By the end of the war, the worldwide banking relationships forged by American Express helped establish customer service offices in every major European city that would continue to aid the traveler.

Coca-Cola, on the other hand, never relinquished its position of popularity, even during times of war. Though distinctive in its flavor, its packaging—the standard soft-drink bottle—was undistinguishable until a decision was made in 1915 to create a new look for Coca-Cola. Thus, the contour-shaped (hourglass) bottle was developed and introduced. Coca-Cola refreshed the masses throughout the war to emerge stronger than ever by the end of the decade. In 1919, the company was sold to a group of investors that included Atlanta banker Ernest Woodruff for $25 million. In a strategic move to replenish those funds, the group immediately took the company public at $40 a share. One share of Coca-Cola, purchased in 1919 with dividends reinvested annually, would be worth between $6 and $7 million today.

> THE AVERAGE annual rate of return on one original share of Coca-Cola at $40, with no additional funds invested other than reinvested dividends, is an astounding 1800% to 2100%.

Coca-Cola fiercely defended its product, trademark, and reputation. In 1920, it brought suit against a company that not only put out a similar product, but played off the company's name, advertising dollars, and reputation. Delivering a decision that would reinforce Coca-Cola's popularity, Supreme Court Justice Oliver Wendell Holmes, Jr., stated, "We are dealing here with a popular drink. . . . well known to the community. . . . The drink characterizes the name as much as the name the drink."[1]

When a company firmly establishes itself in the minds and the hearts of the populace, it can withstand change from within such as financial instability and management change, and pressures from without such as economic growth and war. Such a company is clearly earmarked for longevity. A company with these abilities and qualities, rich in history, with continual growth performance, is a company to consider for long-term investing.

---

[1] 1920.SCT.607, 254 U.S. 143, 65 L. Ed. 189, 41 S. Ct. 113, December 6, 1920, *The Coca-Cola Company* v. *The Koke Company of America*.

CHAPTER NINE

The 1920s

The unforeseen economic benefits of America's brief stint in World War I were that the United States now had overseas territories with access to new markets and abundant raw materials; it also began to lend money abroad. The economy at home also expanded: assembly-line production, easy credit, and broad-based advertising led to mass consumption, which thrust industries into overdrive. The '20s, like the '90s, were a time of excess and expansion.

During the 1920s the masses were introduced to the installment plan, increased their demand and usage of electricity, shopped the new chain stores like A&P, plucked ready-to-wear fashions off the racks, and amassed extensive credit. Consumerism had been born. Demand and product prices pushed upward. But, when wages didn't keep up, Americans fell deeper into debt.

By 1922, the nation was experiencing a dramatic growth spurt. Industry's response was to grow larger corporations that came to dominate many sectors. By the end of the 1920s, one hundred corporations controlled nearly half of the nation's business. This was a decade during which giants were made. The big got bigger and the small got eaten—not unlike the merger-mania of the '90s in which the number of companies shrunk while collective power grew.

What, then, marks this decade thematically for the investor? *Market share acquisition.* Heeding consumer cries, companies learned how to grab the biggest portion of those consumer dollars. Whether through advertising, direct distribution, foreign expansion, or swallowing their competition whole, it was all about gaining market share.

With the auto industry developing new buyers through credit and installment loans, some nine million autos would be on American roads by the end of the decade. The auto industry supported other industries that made steel, glass, rubber, and petroleum, the latter resulting in the formation of new corporations like Gulf Oil and Texaco for the exploration of oil.

The expanding network of highways, funded by state programs, opened up the tourist industry and helped create a new phenomenon, the suburb, which in turn spurred a booming construction industry. With suburban living came more cars and more gas stations to meet expanding consumer demand for speed, ease, and convenience.

New methods of marketing made it easier for the consumer to buy an automobile: manufacturers stimulated sales by extending credit and setting up local car dealerships.

After barely surviving financial ruin, General Motors got back on its feet in 1920 when the DuPont family invested heavily in the company by purchasing stock. Like all large industries at this time, GM leapt forward: By 1924, GM's market share reached 19% of new car sales and it rose again to become market leader by 1926 with 28% of market share; and they established their first European assembly plant.

GM was not only making strides in sales and marketing as stated in CEO Sloan's message to shareholders—"A car for every purse and purpose"—but also in the area of management. GM set a precedent by creating a plan for management to acquire company stock, clearly benefiting stockholders' interests. A company now almost completely vertically and laterally integrated—that produced and assembled its parts, extended credit, offered servicing, and introduced insurance into its financial division—GM continued to expand its reach into Brazil, Argentina, Spain, France, and Germany. Interestingly, one of its greatest strides came through research. GM Research Laboratories introduced ethyl gasoline to the public and developed "knock-less" gasoline, which they marketed in conjunction with Standard Oil of New Jersey (Exxon).

Other companies like Procter and Gamble and Johnson & Johnson (JNJ) expanded internationally in the early '20s, but they also met consumer needs by diversifying their product ranges. JNJ brought out well-known consumer products like the Band-Aid® Brand Bandages and Johnson's Baby Cream. IBM, still known as C-T-R at this time, responded to its international status by changing its name to International Business Machines (IBM). Philip Morris published its first annual report in 1920 and began regular dividend payments in 1928. American Express did not fare as well. As a major holding of Chase National Bank, it was affected by legislation enacted in 1933 (The Banking Act of 1933) that required that banks divest themselves of all non-banking operations. American Express would remain in limbo—not quoted on the market—from the 1929 Crash until the mid to late 1930s.

For companies in the 1920s, growth required an international presence. Those companies taking full advantage of postwar opportunities realized stability—something that would get them through the difficulties that lay ahead. It would be ideal for an investor to be able to predict the future, but that is just not possible. The one thing we can count on is a stock market that rises and falls. So we look for companies with a solid foundation, a management team that is responsive to opportunity, and an investment in its own growth. These companies will weather change.

By the end of the decade, America would face one of its darkest economic events—the 1929 Stock Market Crash. Speculation brought with it a hard-learned lesson. The crash was inevitable. On September 1929, Roger Babson wrote, "Fair weather cannot always continue. The economic cycle is in progress today, as it was in the past. The Federal Reserve System has put the banks in a strong position, but it has not changed human nature. More people are speculating today than ever in our history. Sooner or later a crash is coming and it may be terrific."

On the lighter side, one of my favorite lines about the market just after the crash comes from the 1950 Doris Day movie "Tea For Two," set at the time of the crash. When asked to pay $3.75 for a taxi ride, one character remarked, "$3.75! I can buy AT&T for less."

Here are some of *The New York Times* headlines leading up to the Crash of '29. See if any of these sound similar to recent economic and market reports.

Wednesday, July 3, 1929, Page 31, Col. 5

SEES STOCK RISE JUSTIFIED

Moody's Says Returns Are In Line With Industrial Activity

Friday, September 6, 1929, Page 1, Col. 7

STOCK PRICES BREAK ON DARK PROPHECY

Drop in Hectic Last Hour As Babson's Prediction Of A Big Slump Is Printed

---

Friday, September 6, 1929, Page 12, Col. 2

BABSON PREDICTS 'CRASH' IN STOCKS

Says Wise Investors Will Pay Up Loans and Avoid Marging [sic] Trading

FISHER VIEW IS OPPOSITE

Declares No Big Recession In Market Is Due,
Because Inventions Are Adding to Health

Sunday, October 13, 1929, II, Page 7, Col. 2

STOCK PRICES WILL STAY AT HIGH LEVEL FOR YEARS TO COME, SAYS OHIO ECONOMIST

Wednesday, October 16, 1929, Page 8, Col. 4

FISHER SEES STOCKS PERMANENTLY HIGH

Yale Economist Tells Purchasing Agents Increased Earnings Justify Rise

SAYS TRUST AID SALES

Wednesday, October 16, 1929, Page 41, Col. 1

AYRES SEES MARKET AS 'CREEPING BEAR'

Fall of Prices Began Months Ago, He Says, But Was Hidden by Rising Averages

DECLINE IN AUTUMN USUAL

Recession This Season About 14 Per Cent, Against Normal Drop of 9, He Reports

Wednesday, October 16, 1929, Page 41, Col. 4

MITCHELL ASSERTS STOCKS ARE SOUND

Banker, Sailing From Europe, Says He Sees No Signs of Wall Street Slump

Tuesday, October 22, 1929, Page 24, Col. 1

FISHER SAYS PRICES OF STOCKS ARE LOW

Quotations Have Not Caught Up With Real Values As Yet, He Declares

SEES NO CAUSE FOR SLUMP

Economist Tells Credit Men that Market Has Not Been Inflated, But Merely Readjusted

Wednesday, October 23, 1929, Page 1, Col. 4

STOCKS GAIN SHARPLY BUT SLIP NEAR CLOSE

Vigorous Recovery Marks Most of Day and Many Issues Show Net Advances

MARKET GLOOM LESSENED

Banking Support, Ease of Money and Mitchell's Optimistic Statement Help Rally

Thursday, October 24, 1929, Page 1, Col. 1

PRICES OF STOCKS CRASH IN HEAVY LIQUIDATION, TOTAL DROP OF BILLIONS

PAPER LOSS $4,000,000,000

2,600,000 Shares Sold In the Final Hour In Record Decline

MANY ACCOUNTS WIPED OUT

But No Brokerage House Is In Difficulties, As Margins Have Been Kept High

ORGANIZED BANKING ABSENT

Bankers Confer on Steps To Support Market – Highest Break Is 96 Points

Thursday, October 24, 1929, Page 2, Col. 1

SAYS STOCK SLUMP IS ONLY TEMPORARY

Professor Fisher Tells Capital Bankers Market Rise Since War Has Been Justified

ECONOMIC REASONS CITED

"Public Speculative Mania," He Declares, is Least Important Cause of Price Inflation

---

Saturday, October 26, 1929, Page 2, Col. 5

CAUTION ADVISED BY STOCK BROKERS

Letters to Clients Warn Against Hysterical Selling and Favor Some Buying

TONE IS OPTIMISTIC

Narrow Trading is Predicted for a Time
Till the Market Recuperates

Tuesday, October 29, 1929, Page 1, Col. 6

STOCK PRICES SLUMP $14,000,000,000 IN NATION-WIDE STAMPEDE TO UNLOAD; BANKERS TO SUPPORT MARKET TODAY

Sixteen Leading Issues Down $2,893,520,108; Tel. & Tel. And Steel Among Heaviest Losses

---

PREMIER ISSUES HARD HIT

Unexpected Torrent of Liquidation
Again Rocks Markets

Wednesday, October 30, 1929, Page 1, Columns 6-8

STOCKS COLLAPSE IN 16,400,030-SHARE DAY, BUT RALLY AT CLOSE CHEERS BROKERS; BANKERS OPTIMISTIC, TO CONTINUE AID

---

240 Issues Lose $15,894,818,894 in Month; Slump in Full Exchange List Vastly Larger

CHAPTER TEN

The Great Depression

In the Great Depression, the American Dream collapsed into desperation. Those bedrock values of democracy, capitalism, and individualism were being questioned; Hollywood screen dreams became the hope for a better life for much of the United States. Between 1929 and 1932 the income of the average American family dropped by 40%. New, developing businesses collapsed, banks failed, and survival replaced any thought of economic advancement.

At the consumer level, luxuries disappeared and everyone tried to put new life into old things. First, people got rid of telephones; then they stopped buying furniture, appliances, jewelry, and candy. In contrast, sales of gasoline, radios, refrigerators, and cigarettes stayed strong. The strongest overall sales record came from Hollywood movies—escapism from personal despair became a national pastime.

Looking at the stock market during those Depression years reveals an interesting perspective for the individual investor. In September of 1929 when stock prices began to fluctuate, most viewed these variations as a temporary situation and expected the market would adjust itself. They did not recognize that when profits fail to support unrealistic stock prices, it should be taken as a warning sign. Rapidly declining sales of goods and ever increasing stock prices further signaled the oncoming failure. Since most believed that a market in upswing mode was reflective of a healthy and growing economy and that Adam Smith's 150-year-old theory of laissez-faire economics held true, nothing could change that—at least nothing as dramatic as the events of October, 1929.

On October 24, 1929, known as "Black Thursday," nerves were rattled and investors began dumping their stocks as quickly as they could. Even the efforts of financiers like J.P. Morgan to help stabilize the market by buying stocks failed by opening bell on Monday morning. Sell orders flooded the floor and by Black Tuesday, October 29, 1929, the market plummeted to depths it had never before seen. $30 billion was lost.

With public confidence at an all-time low, attitudes about the state of the economy ran the gamut. Former President Coolidge lamented, "This country is not in good condition," while John D. Rockefeller optimistically replied, ". . . Depressions have come and gone. Prosperity has always returned and will again." And both were right.

Though a pall hung over the land, Philip Morris viewed this period as an opportune time to expand. While prices for materials and real estate were low, they made acquisitions and diversified, purchasing a plant in Richmond, Virginia, where they would manufacture their own cigarettes. By 1934, as the nation began to regain its economic foothold, Philip Morris had risen head and shoulders above disaster. They had also successfully launched six new products, such as the ivory-tipped Marlboro, filter tip Parliament, and their domestic-Turkish tobacco blend. They continued to advertise on radio and made Johnny the bell-hop and his "Call for Philip Morr-ay-us" phrase recognized nationwide. Philip Morris had chosen the Rockefeller attitude to drive them through desperate times.

Automotive manufacturers, including GM, faced the 1929 Crash by consolidation and stepping up competition. With fewer players on the field, the Big Three survived and even thrived by incorporating a standard volume concept. Using a financial strategy that endures today, GM set its prices to produce a 20 percent return on investment based on the average year's sales. So, when sales soared, GM saw its profits rise as well. Though car sales were in the millions, GM's corporate survival strategy created a long-term mandate that had helped them through the lean years.

Coca-Cola's survival during the Depression years can be credited largely to the nature of their business. While other companies were scrambling for profits, Coca-Cola successfully operated 64 bottling operations in 28 countries. Considered entertainment rather than a luxury, Coke continued to sell in high volumes. "The Pause That Refreshes," as first seen in the Saturday Evening Post, became a cause for profit. Coca-Cola's pre-Crash stock price was a meteoric $171.50, paying a dividend of $5.75. The 1929 Crash reduced the stock to $133.75 with a reduced dividend. The years between 1931 and 1933 were difficult times for companies: Coca-Cola did see a lowering of the stock's value, but it continued to pay healthy dividends; it saw a rise again of the stock's value in 1934 to $161.50 and split the stock four-for-one in 1935.

Procter & Gamble kept America clean. Ivory Soap, a staple in American bathrooms, remained a profitable item during the Depression years. Advertising directly to the consumer and sponsoring daytime radio dramas in 1932 (hence, the "Soap Opera") kept the product's name at the forefront and the product in demand. P&G's first TV commercial aired in 1939 for its #1 product—Ivory Soap. Aside from providing loyal customers with needed products, P&G initiated a voluntary profit-sharing program to help employees weather economic stress.

The Chinese say that with disaster comes opportunity. This adage very much reflects how giants continued to stand tall in knee-buckling times. In the early days of the Great Depression, the Dow was depressed as well, but by mid-decade began to regain its footing. Though the market didn't rebound to its previous high of 300 in 1928, or post-Crash figure of 248 until the 1950s, the Dow moved steadily upward during that time. This is a clear indication that investors were back in the market, buying at the bottom and steadily building.

Companies were devastated by the mass selling of stocks that crashed the market, but many hung on and used this opportunity to build their businesses. Though investors (or even analysts, for that matter) can never predict bottom, we also know that beaten-down stocks can deliver gains, especially when they are backed by high-quality companies that dominate their industry, have a diverse customer base, and pay high dividends. These high-yielding stocks (% yield = dividend ÷ stock price) are referred to as the "Dogs of the Dow" and are considered good values. Here's an excerpt from *The Wall Street Journal* of January 2, 2001, concerning this issue:

Philip Morris Leads 'Dogs of Dow' Pack

NEW YORK—As it has been for most of the year, Philip Morris Cos. was the highest-yielding issue in the Dow Jones Industrial Average at year end, leading the so-called Dogs of the Dow list. . . .

The "dogs" for 2000—Philip Morris, J.P. Morgan & Co., Eastman Kodak Co., Caterpillar Inc., and General Motors Corp.—outperformed the 30 DJIA stocks as a whole, rising more than 6%, while the Dow Jones Industrial Average fell 6.2%.

CHAPTER ELEVEN

World War II

Worrld War II substantially defined the 1940s. Just bouncing back from the Depression era, corporate America shifted its focus away from consumerism and expansion into war-defined needs. Automobile production ceased in 1942 so that tanks, ships, and planes could be built to support the war in Europe and elsewhere. Gasoline and food were carefully rationed to help provide the troops with what they needed; and Americans organized "scrap drives" for steel, tin, copper, and rubber. Before the war, British and German inventors had been working on jet aircraft. These efforts were placed on hold; it wasn't until postwar 1948 that the first operational jet fighter appeared from Boeing. Although television had made its debut in 1939, further development ceased until the early 1950s.

The first digital computer made its debut in the early '40s: ENIAC appeared unofficially in 1945, stood 10 feet tall and weighed 30 tons (the 1957 Tracy/Hepburn movie *Desk Set* portrayed the computer monstrosity perfectly). It used over 70,000 resistors, 10,000 capacitors, 6,000 switches, and 18,000 vacuum tubes and enough wattage to light a town. The use of tubes, replacing switches and relays, was an important advancement: additions were performed in 200 microseconds, multiplication in 3 milliseconds, and division in 30 milliseconds. This is slow by today's standards, but when the Navy needed quick and accurate computations for artillery firing charts, ENIAC could account for wind and elevation in its split-second calculations.

As the United States moved to a wartime economy, mobilization took place quickly. Unlike WWI, when there was no previous model, America in the 1940s knew how to respond. This period also marks

America's debut as the world's largest weapons manufacturer and economic power. New industries also emerged due to military needs,
such as for synthetic rubber. And new industries arose to meet
wartime necessities, such as the frozen TV dinner.

Americans now experienced full employment and higher earnings. They worked hard, but they played hard, too: Big Band music,
crooners, and the jitterbug were all the rage; listening to the radio was
family entertainment; and Hollywood was in its heyday when the government declared movies essential for morale.

Crop prices rose, production increased, and farm income tripled.
Corporate America flourished as both consumers and companies
united in the war effort. The ability of companies to re-define themselves for a short-term need had two results: the short-term need was
successfully met and the process of meeting that need created new
products—a "new market" boon that would see its flowering in the
prosperous '50s. Many companies earned government issued medals
for their war effort.

Philip Morris's history during the 1940s shows that the war years
were a winch-down period for the company. Except for the purchase
of one plant facility in Louisville, Kentucky, everything remained at
the status quo. But, in the wake of American victory, Philip Morris
geared for accelerated growth.

Coca-Cola, by contrast, found itself in high productivity mode for
its product during the war. As part of the war effort in 1941, the head
of the Coca-Cola Company promised a price cap of five cents for anyone in uniform, no matter what the cost. In 1943, General Eisenhower
sent a telegram to the Coca-Cola Company requesting 3 million bottles
of the liquid gold to quench the thirst of his troops, along with 10
bottling plants complete with facilities to wash, refill, and cap more
product twice a month. It isn't uncommon to see a Coca-Cola truck in
WWII photos. Still ever protective of its trademark, and after using the
word "Coke" alongside Coca-Cola in advertising since 1941, the company registered "Coke" as a trademark in 1945. The Coca-Cola Company sponsored family-time radio shows and when TV came into full
swing by the end of the war, it would sponsor the first live network
TV show with ventriloquist Edgar Bergen and his communicative side-
kick Charlie McCarthy. Coca-Cola's stock price, though briefly dip-

ping in 1941, regained stability. The $5.00 dividend the company paid in 1941 was rolled back to $4.00 during the war years, reinstated to $5 after the war and paid $6 in 1949. The average annual closing price for Coca-Cola stock during the '40s was $132.45.

The automobile industry would seem to have been hit the hardest. Metal and gasoline were needed to support the overseas war effort, so by 1942 the very last passenger car rolled off the U.S. assembly lines until the end of the war. All production was converted to wartime manufacturing of shells, bombs, machine guns, navigational equipment, and war vehicles. General Motors, for example, went from producing its 25 millionth car in 1940 to ceasing all consumer-based production. This didn't mean that they shut down. It simply meant that they had a different buyer of goods. During the war, GM delivered over $12.3 billion worth of goods to be used for the Allied effort, providing them with the resources for retooling to meet the postwar need for speed, power, and style.

America's home health needs didn't cease. In 1941, JNJ's established suture business grew into its own division. Its personal products division, which included Modess Sanitary Napkins, Red Cross, Band-Aids, assorted baby products, floss and toothbrushes, continued in sales. And JNJ's contribution to the war effort won them the Army/Navy "E Flag" Medal. To provide the government with tin it needed, JNJ changed their Band-Aid packaging from tin boxes to paper boxes. Products sold to the military were simply wrapped in plain brown paper with the product's name—no advertising, no logo, nothing. Like all other companies, they were assigned the manufacture of weaponry. JNJ manufactured artillery shells and gas masks. When the government needed a strong, waterproof tape that could easily be ripped in the fields, JNJ developed "DUCK" tape, which would come to be known during the '50s construction boom as "DUCT" tape. Though the Johnson and Johnson Company archives indicate that they paid a modest dividend during the war, ever since the company went public on September 25, 1944, they have consistently paid a dividend.

IBM had already begun working on the computer in the '40s, but the outbreak of war placed all IBM facilities at the disposal of the government. Their product line expanded to more than three-dozen ordinance items including bombsights, rifles and engine parts. CEO Watson also made an interesting management decision at this time. He invoiced the government at a nominal one percent above cost. This helped ensure that overhead expenses such as wages and materials were covered, but, more importantly, he used that one percent profit to establish a widows and orphans fund.

The need for government applications helped accelerate IBM's growth. They continued their work in the area of computing with the first Automatic Sequence Controlled Calculator, the Mark I, in 1944. Their continuing research helped position them as a new technology market leader as the new decade approached.

Though war also changed life on the home front, people had already been used to doing without many luxuries because of the Depression. War did, however, power industries into full strength and put people back to work. With World War I as a model, industries knew what their roles would be and were ready to deliver. More importantly, companies were still able to continue their research and commitment to new production once the war was over, helping to create an expansion not seen since the Second Industrial Revolution.

Continuing commitment to product development and readiness to act at a moment's notice placed many of the giants on the fast track for growth. Investors in value stocks continued to see their portfolios grow as well.

CHAPTER TWELVE

The 1950s

The end of World War II brought American servicemen home, imbued with hope and confidence. America felt invincible and the authority structure was regarded as a benevolent father. With energy never before seen, American industry expanded to meet peacetime needs. Available to consumers was a new crop of goods not available during the war. A desire for new, more, and better products created corporate expansion and jobs. Growth permeated every aspect of the '50s lifestyle; even babies were booming.

At this time, the industries in the forefront of American production were auto, oil, aircraft, chemicals, and electronics. As the passenger car resumed manufacture in 1946, demand exceeded supply, stretching productivity levels to a new high, but costs were kept at bay by continuous automation upgrades. GM gave the consumer bigger, flashier cars with chrome, tailfins, automatic transmissions, and powerful V-8 engines. Car sales sped from 4.8 million in 1949 to nearly 7.22 million in 1955. By the end of this decade the public would be clamoring for a sportier, more compact car. The DuPont family money that once helped save GM from financial ruin was now deemed by the U.S. Supreme Court a violation of the Clayton Antitrust Act: as Directors, the DuPonts held too much stock—some 23%.

Oil replaced coal as the nation's standard source of energy. The aircraft companies, like Boeing, were propelled into space research and commercial jet airliners through their previous wartime defense research. The chemical industry brought the public new products made of plastics and synthetic fibers. Americans wore the "new" polyester fabrics. The computer began to change the business model as technology strived to match the consumer thirst for innovation.

IBM, no longer constricted by wartime work and research, used the knowledge they gained to advance the computer. In 1952, IBM introduced its first vacuum tube computer, an important advancement in business applications used for billing, payroll, and inventory control. IBM led data processing in a new direction with its Random Access Method of Accounting and Control (RAMAC), the first computer disc storage system and a new computer language. By 1959, the transistor, originally used in the radio, replaced the vacuum tube. The computer was on its way to becoming more powerful, more capable, and smaller. Hewlett-Packard, too, saw a dramatic rise in the need for technology. Their testing equipment sales tripled during the war and with continuing postwar expansion the company went public in 1957.

New industries arose from the wartime effort, which now created new opportunities. Employment was high. Incomes were on the rise. The size of the middle class was now doubled (the 76 million babies born certainly helped contribute to this statistic). Money was plentiful and Americans were willing to spend it. Three out of five families in America paid mortgages instead of rent; by the end of the decade, most families watched television and everyone used credit cards and bought on the installment plan. Debt was a new by-product of consumer zeal.

In the corporate sector, companies created new ways to attract consumer dollars: they couldn't throw advertising dollars at the TV networks fast enough. When the consumer began to demand a faster, easier lifestyle, companies analyzed how to ramp up their current delivery systems: they made their services and products more readily available to the consumer by opening local branch offices and franchises. The postwar '50s boom redefined consumer needs and American tastes and brought with it the first McDonald's and cookie-cutter franchises in 1955.

Companies now began to expand by bringing together unrelated industries, forming huge conglomerates, or by crushing or buying out their competition. Foreign expansion meant not just exporting, but setting up plants in resource-rich areas. Many, like Hewlett-Packard and Philip Morris, spread the wealth through profit-sharing programs for their employees in the '50s, making companies like these more attractive to work for and to invest in.

Philip Morris launched its newest icon: a weather-beaten cowboy—the Marlboro Man. Like all big companies in the '50s, Philip Morris vied for its share of TV advertising and walked away with the first sponsorship of a National Football League telecast. Philip Morris's production not only accelerated but it capitalized on a "larger-than-life" American mindset, and reflected it in company names, icons, and labeling: the "Commander," "Alpine," and of course, the Marlboro Man.

Coca-Cola came out with king-size and family-size bottles befitting a booming population and launched the orange soft drink Fanta.

Ray Kroc, originally the franchise agent for the McDonald Brothers in 1954, opened two restaurants in 1955, totaling the year out at $193,772. By the end of 1957, there were some 40 restaurants with total sales of nearly $4 million. In 1958, McDonald's sold its 100 millionth hamburger and had sales surpassing $10 million. In just one decade, Americans would know to look for the all-familiar golden arches landmark; they represented and created part of the surge in the food industry.

The golden decade of the '50s is best summed up by Charles Wilson, then President of General Motors: while being considered for the position of Secretary of Defense, he commented, ". . . for years I thought that what was good for our country was good for General Motors, and vice versa."

Investors love boom times. Everyone does well. There is money to be made from emerging industries and growth companies. The wise investor, though, doesn't put all of his or her eggs in one basket. When a new technology emerges, it is always best to ascertain how much you can comfortably invest in risk-laden stocks. Always mindful that these companies will not be paying dividends, it is best to balance your portfolio with value, low-risk companies that will continue to grow, even in down times, and pay dividends. Also, with emerging industries, evolving companies come in two flavors: leaders and laggards. The leaders will generally win in the end and will either swallow or squash the wannabees. Which company would you rather invest in?

WHEN CONSIDERING a stock for investment, the NAIC suggests that a company have at least a five-year history of sales and earnings on which you can base an opinion about the company's future and make an investment decision.

CHAPTER THIRTEEN

The 1960s

If the 1950s represented innovation and post-war prosperity, the 1960s are perhaps best defined by expansion and liberalism. The reflective mood was "revolution." Business as usual was being challenged and, in the corporate world, this translated into "change or die."

As Americans demanded "affirmative action," established companies sought "affirming action"—products and services in tune with consumers asserting their right to safety and value. From an economic viewpoint, the '60s was a swing decade between the authority-embracing prosperity of the '50s and the self-absorbed excesses of the '70s. Those complacent, optimistic giants from the previous decade's booming economy struggled against the boom being lowered on all companies. Clear vision in the eye of chaos defines how these giants prevailed during the '60s.

Technology stocks were in full run on the market. New, exciting, high-priced and risky, many peaked in 1968 and tanked by 1970. From *Dun's Magazine* (1971), Table 13.1 is a list of some of Wall Street's "hot" technology stocks from 1968. Though some of these names may be familiar, only Electronic Data is still around today. More importantly, look at the extremely high price-to-earnings ratios.

Expansion was still the theme of the day, and Philip Morris identified the newer area of overseas trade alliances in 1960. Continuing through 1962, Philip Morris embraced Hong Kong, France, Mexico, Guatemala, Finland, Sweden and Italy as trade partners—thus moving toward a balance between domestic and foreign business. New avenues of sponsorship linked them to the popular "CBS Reports,"

TABLE 13.1

Company	1968 High	1970 Low	% drop	P/E at High
Fairchild Camera	$102.00	$18.00	–82%	443
Teledyne	72.00	13.00	–82	42
Control Data	163.00	28.00	–83	54
Mohawk Data	111.00	18.00	–84	285
Electronic Data	162.00	24.00	–85	352
Optical Scanning	146.00	16.00	–89	200
Itek	172.00	17.00	–90	71
University Computing	186.00	13.00	–93	118

successfully placing them in the national eye. Then in 1963, they launched what continues today as a benchmark advertising campaign for tobacco—"Marlboro Country." The Marlboro cigarette thus became an icon of masculine America, attracting a solid consumer base: if not hippies and revolutionaries, then cowboys. By 1968, the introduction of "Virginia Slims" offered a similar cachet for women.

Philip Morris was carefully carving out niches in a volatile consumer market: even against the January 1964 Surgeon General's Report on "Smoking and Health." Working for balance, by March Philip Morris had introduced the charcoal filter. The giant was responsive and quick, gleaning continued success and pocketing over $1 billion in revenues in 1968.

General Motors (GM) faced its own set of challenges during the '60s—in particular, consumer-driven issues of safety and size. Quickly responding in 1960 to the demands for a smaller, more economical car, GM gave America the Corvair. GM also introduced several more models in each of their lines in 1961: the Buick Special, Oldsmobile F-85, and Pontiac Tempest. By 1962, they had added the Chevy II. America responded positively because in that same year, the number of GM shareholders exceeded one million.

GM was looking strong with its impressive array of small cars. Then in 1965 Ralph Nader's book, *Unsafe at Any Speed* targeted the popular Corvair as unsafe. GM listened and responded with several new safety features in their vehicles, including rear seat shoulder belts.

No longer holding its sales record, the Corvair was discontinued in 1969. But GM had not reached its outer limits in 1969—it was now reaching for outer space. Responsible for the manufacture of the guidance and navigation systems that guided the Apollo 11 astronauts, they landed on the moon and returned home. Throughout the '60s, GM had been quick to act and counteract. They held on to 48% of the market share for automobiles (compared to 28% in 2001) and reigned victorious in space by the end of the decade.

Coca-Cola continued to quench the thirsty masses, but now it would add something new to reach the new crop of those who were health conscious: Minute Maid Orange Juice came on board. "Soda" never fell out of favor, though. During the 1950s' Korean Conflict, the Coca-Cola Company once again quenched the troops' thirst. This time, they shipped the product in durable, unbreakable aluminum cans. In 1960, the "can" was introduced to the public. With the purchase of the Minute Maid Company came a citrus resource and, in 1961, the fresh, new lemon-lime drink, Sprite, found its way into the hands of the mature, urbane Coke drinker as did TAB, the company's low-calorie answer for the diet conscious. The company's 1963 slogan, "Things go better with Coke," placed Coca-Cola on the dinner table as an accompaniment, displacing healthier options. I know I spent my college years supplementing dorm food with pizza, potato chips, Mallomars, and Coke.

The baby-boomer generation entered restless, uncertain times during the '60s. Their causes changed, their drink of choice may have changed, but they certainly seemed to benefit the Coca-Cola Company with their ability to change with the times. Even with the number two soft-drink company breathing down their necks, they remained on top and ". . . the real thing."

The fast food industry also re-established its position during the '60s. Hamburgers became an obsession and McDonald's was the place to "hang out." Anywhere you went, you could "Look for the Golden Arches" and get the all-American meal—a hamburger, fries, and a milkshake. Not having a lengthy history, as did other giants, didn't hurt this industry forerunner. In 1961, Ray Kroc bought out the McDonald

Brothers and positioned the company for amazing growth: McDonald's leapt from its 400 millionth hamburger in 1960 to 700 million in 1962 and one billion in 1963 (beat out only by the forty-year-old White Castle that claimed its one billionth hamburger sale in 1961). The crimson coiffed clown, Ronald McDonald (as first played by NBC weatherman Willard Scott), made his debut in 1965 to spread the word. Hamburgers made their way onto TV and McDonald's (MCD) hit the NYSE in 1966. This investment influx gave McDonald's the impetus to open restaurants internationally and, by the end of the decade, 5 billion hamburgers had been consumed worldwide.

For large companies like McDonald's, challenge brings change. Where new needs emerge, new products must be ready to meet those needs. That's why every company spends a portion of its revenues on some form of research, consumer or otherwise. That is not to say that every product will be greeted by consumers with open arms, but a company's challenge is to continue research and development.

While the giants were growing, another newcomer on the scene would soon walk among them. As Americans became more fiscally conscious, Sam Walton was convinced that he could collect a piece of the retail pie by offering a wide array of merchandise at reduced prices. He opened his first Wal-Mart store in Arkansas in 1962, offering up goods with a smile. By the end of the decade, Wal-Mart was incorporated, was publicly traded by 1970, offered profit-sharing, stock options, and employee discounts, and was on its way to becoming a household name. By the time Sam Walton died in 1992 as the second richest man in the world, Wal-Mart was already the number one retailer in the nation.

For Wal-Mart, chaotic times and the consumer fed an inspiration. Fiscal success came with the implementation of marketing, growth through acquisition, and an eventual international presence. What is important for the investor to realize is that there will always be new models for success in every industry, as well as new industries in our age of technology. But when we stay tuned-in to our times, ask questions, keep reading about and following the newest innovations, think about whether the consumer's needs are aptly being considered and satisfied either as a primary purpose or result of business, we will find companies that will prove their worth and be worthy investments.

CHAPTER FOURTEEN

The 1970s–1980s

We view these two decades between 1970 and 1990 as one unit because they are so strongly linked economically. Looking back at this time, one sees a period of narcissism followed by excess and implosion. Much like the relationship between the '20s and '30s, the climax of that 20-year period was meltdown. Before looking at companies that both survived and evolved during that time, it will be helpful to look at the bigger cultural picture in America.

During the 1930s, the environment became a major problem—eroded land could not sustain farming, grazing, or even forestry. This problem was especially acute in the South and East Texas, and portions of Oklahoma, New Mexico, Colorado, and Kansas. The breadbasket of America was empty and Panhandle dust reached as far as the Atlantic and Gulf coasts. Soil conservation and replenishment became a national priority. In the '80s, environmental issues extended to acid rain, oil spills, the greenhouse effect, endangered species, and an ozone layer that was becoming depleted.

For both the '30s and '80s, crime and economic problems were the other two areas of concern. Where mobs and bank robbers characterized the '30s, the '80s witnessed international drug trafficking and a globalized mob. The solutions for crimes of the '80s depended heavily on international cooperation.

Economic problems in the '80s also extended beyond America's borders. While the federal government ran its largest deficit ever, consumer demand for imported goods transformed the United States into a debtor nation. Borrowing had reached critical mass.

If you look then at the climate of the decade just before the '80s, you see a 1970s' disillusionment with government, civil rights demands, women's movements, environmental concerns, and a concerted drive to explore space.

The '70s also saw the arrival of the floppy disc and the microprocessor—"computer on a chip." Technology had birthed a new revolution of toys, biological research, and travel. This was the decade that saw the first test tube baby and jumbo jets.

Specific to big business and consumer investing, how is it that some fared well, even spectacularly, while others crashed and burned? The timeline below shows the bigger corporate picture between 1970 and 1987, using Philip Morris as a benchmark for weathering change. What you see as you scan down those years is adaptability and diversification. It would seem that Philip Morris understood well the climate of the '70s and '80s and responded with astute corporate decisions. This is important information for an investor—companies whose stocks will yield dependably over a long period of time are those responsive to cultural trends and events. Today, despite litigation and other setbacks, Philip Morris is still—as measured by its standing in the economy—a giant.

We begin with 1970 and highlight events that show responsiveness to the changes during these two decades.

1970—Philip Morris Incorporated acquires 100% of Miller Brewing Company.

February—Marlboro 100's red pack test-marketed in Seattle and Spokane, Washington.

December—Plainwell Paper Company, Inc., acquired by Philip Morris Industrial.

—Cigarette companies voluntarily agree to display "tar" and nicotine data in all advertising.

* * *

1971—Oscar Mayer & Company becomes the first major meat processor to use open dating on packages.

January—Ban on advertising cigarettes on television and radio goes into effect.

* * *

1972

January—Cigarette manufacturers are required to include health warnings on all advertising, direct mail, and point-of-sale material.

—Marlboro Lights introduced.

—Parliament 100's with charcoal filter go national.

April—Philip Morris celebrates its 125th anniversary.

December—License agreement signed with Japan Tobacco and Salt Public Corporation and Federal Tobacco Ltd., Trinidad and Tobago, for the manufacture of Marlboros.

—Marlboro ends the year as the world's best-selling cigarette.

* * *

1974

January—Miller announces record sales for 1973, moving it from seventh to fifth place in the industry, and plans a $70 million brewery in Fulton, New York.

October—Johnny, 40-year spokesman for Philip Morris, retires. (He was famous for the phrase "Call For Philip Morris!")

December—Miller and Lowenbrau sign licensing agreement.

* * *

1975—*Miller begins to brew and market a domestic Lowenbrau.*

January—Philip Morris Inc.'s 1974 operating revenues surpass $3 billion.

March—Lite Beer from Miller introduced nationally.

December—Dun & Bradstreet's Review cites Philip Morris as "one of the five best-managed companies by 1976."

* * *

1977

—Merit 100's introduced nationally.

—Philip Morris Inc. announces that it again had record earnings for 1976, and its consolidated operating revenues for the year exceeded $4 billion for the first time. The company registered the U.S. cigarette industry's largest gain in unit sales and increased its U.S. market share to 25.1%.

—The international company's share of the cigarette market outside the United States rose to 5.1%.

February—Wisconsin Tissue Mills acquired by Philip Morris Industrial.

* * *

1978

May–June—Philip Morris Inc. announces a tender offer for The Seven-Up Company, and subsequently reaches an understanding with the management of Seven-Up for the combination of the two companies. As a result of the tender offer, Philip Morris acquires 97% of Seven-Up common stock and merges Seven-Up into a wholly-owned subsidiary that assumes the Seven-Up name. Seven-Up now becomes the sixth Philip Morris operating company.

June—Philip Morris Inc. buys the international cigarette business of the Liggett Group Inc.

* * *

1979

September—Philip Morris Inc. and Miller Brewing Company officially open Central New York Bottle Company in Auburn, New York. Plans are announced to invest an additional $15 million to increase capacity from its present 720 million containers annually to 990 million annually.

—Miller announces the start of aluminum-can manufacturing at its Reidsville, North Carolina, plant.

* * *

1980—*Oscar Mayer & Co. purchases a plant in Sandusky, Ohio, for its quick-frozen and prepared food products for its consumer, food service, and specialty sales divisions.*

—Post Fruit & Fibre cereal placed on market by General Foods Corporation.

June—Construction begins on a $17 million soft-drink production/distribution center for Seven-Up Bottling of Houston, a division of The Seven-Up Company.

August—Seven-Up acquires the Seven-Up Bottling Company of Albuquerque, New Mexico, Inc.

October—Seven-Up acquires Oxnard Lemon Company.

November—Production of L&M cigarettes begins at Canton, Ohio's number-two cigarette factory.

* * *

1981—*General Foods Corporation acquires Oscar Mayer & Co.*

January—Miller reports that 37.3 million barrels of beer were shipped in 1980, a 4.2% increase over 1979. Lite beer became the third largest-selling brand in the United States.

—For the 27th consecutive year, Philip Morris Inc. announces record revenues and earnings, as consolidated operating revenues increased to $9.8 billion. The company again registered a record increase in unit sales, increasing its domestic market share to 31%. The international company's share of the cigarette market outside the U.S. rose to 6.2%.

* * *

1982—*Philip Morris Credit Corporation is incorporated.*

—Entenmann's, Inc., is acquired by General Foods Corporation.

—Philip Morris Inc. announces record revenues and earnings for the 28th consecutive year, as consolidated operating revenues increased to $10.9 billion. For the 15th consecutive year, the company registered the U.S. cigarette industry's largest gain in unit sales, increasing its U.S. market share to 31.8%. The international company's share of the cigarette market outside the U.S. rose to about 6.4%.

February—Philip Morris Credit Corporation is incorporated.

—Philip Morris Incorporated begins sponsorship of the Joffrey Ballet.

—The Seven-Up Company unveils a "No Caffeine" advertising campaign for its 7UP brand.

August—The Seven-Up Company begins to roll out Like Cola across the United States; first expansion market is Detroit.

—Philip Morris Industrial sells the three companies that comprised the Chemical Group—Polymer Industries, Armstrong Products Co., and Polymer Chemie GmbH.

—The Miller Brewing Company's successful "Miller Time" advertising campaign is broadened to "Welcome to Miller Time."

October—The Seven-Up Company introduces Sugar Free Like Cola in six test markets.

November—Philip Morris U.S.A. announces a $617,000 grant to the University of Kentucky for the support of barley production research.

* * *

1983

October—The Seven-Up Company renames 10 company-owned bottling operations 7UP/Like Cola Bottling companies.

—The Seven-Up Company opens the 7UP Consumer Center, a nationwide toll-free consumer response system, the first in the soft-drink industry.

—The Seven-Up Company adds NutraSweet to Diet 7UP and Sugar Free Like Cola in selected markets.

—Philip Morris Inc. announces that it will purchase, from time to time over the next year, up to four million shares of its common stock in the open market or in privately negotiated transactions.

* * *

1984—Miller Brewing Company enters selected test markets with two new beers: Sharp's LA, the company's first low-alcohol product, and Meister Brau Light.

October—Miller introduces a new premium beer—Plank Road Original Draught—in five test markets. The beer is a draft beer, but is packaged and sold in 12-ounce bottles rather than in traditional kegs.

* * *

1985—Philip Morris Companies Inc. acquires General Foods Corporation.

—Philip Morris International's volume grew 5.5% to 258.2 billion units. Miller Brewing Company shipments totaled 37.52 million barrels. The Seven-Up Company reported a 12.9% gain in revenues, to $734 million.

—The Miller Brewing Company introduces a new marketing plan for Miller High Life, "Miller—Made the American Way," and brings back the majestic eagle emblem.

August—General Foods Corporation introduces the Fresh Lock packet for coffee. The packet removes all air and moisture from the container, allowing the coffee to remain fresher longer.

* * *

1986—Philip Morris Companies Inc. sells Seven-Up International, the third-largest soft drink company outside of the U.S., and Seven-Up Canada to PepsiCo.

> July—Miller Brewing Company becomes a first-tier subsidiary of the Philip Morris Companies Inc.

* * *

1987—General Foods three business sectors become three separate operating companies: General Foods, USA; General Foods, Coffee & International; and Oscar Mayer Foods.

> January—Philip Morris Companies Inc. announces 1986 consolidated operating revenues increased 59.2% to $25.4 billion. Net earnings were up 17.7% to $1.5 billion, from the prior year's net earnings of $1.3 billion. Earnings per share were $6.20 up 18.3% from $5.24 in 1985. The 1986 results include General Foods Corporation, a wholly-owned subsidiary since November 1, 1985, and exclude The Seven-Up Company.
>
> —Philip Morris Credit Corporation (PMCC), an unconsolidated subsidiary, had revenues of $162.0 million, an increase of 74%; while net earnings rose 100%, to $70.9 million. These results include the equity income since July 1986 of Mission Viejo Realty Group Inc., PMCC's real estate subsidiary.

What we see in this timeline is both a monthly and yearly decision-making process. Responsive to changing times, even within very short periods, PM took action as needed to reshape the company and maximize profitability.

Creating new brands, acquiring new product lines, expanding globally, advertising and marketing, and community endeavors are all signs of a company that thinks forward and evolves outward.

Let's now move from Philip Morris to the automobile industry and General Motors (GM).

For most U.S. automakers, revenues declined sharply in the '70s and '80s as Americans declared their search for smaller, more fuel-efficient cars. The VW Beetle had become a bug that was challenging American ideas about car design and performance. While companies like Chrysler teetered on the edge of bankruptcy, GM began looking beyond its national borders for a solution, forging an alliance with Suzuki and Isuzu. By the year 2000, GM would have added investment stakes in Fiat, Ferrari, Lancia, and Maserati. During the '70s, GM focused its attention on smaller cars that met pollution control guidelines and conserved on gas. In 1984, GM and Toyota formed NUMMI in order to bring Japanese auto building technology into the U.S. since alliances and adaptability were hallmarks of this period. Again, the timeline below exhibits the weave of GM's momentum during this time. This is what we look for in a giant. Reading a timeline gives the investor a more complete picture of the company that you may not always get from an annual report.

1970

—GM forms a five-member Public Policy Committee.

1. A two-phase automotive emissions control program directed to encourage use of unleaded gasoline in the U.S. is announced by Edward Cole, President of GM.

2. GM introduces no lead or low lead tolerant engines on all of its 1971 models in the U.S. and Canada.

3. Industrial air and water pollution control programs are announced at a General Motors news conference.

—GM production in the U.S. is halted by a 10-week United Auto Workers (UAW) strike, beginning on September 15.

* * *

1971

—GM forms an Environmental Activities Staff to concentrate on the performance of GM products in the environment.

—A Science Advisory Committee, consisting of top scientists selected from across the U.S., is formed to advise the GM Executive Committee on policies and activities concerning basic and applied research.

—GM designs and manufactures the mobility system for the Lunar Roving Vehicle, which enables Apollo 15 astronauts to accomplish mankind's first vehicular drive on the moon.

* * *

1972

—A new combined lap and shoulder belt system with both a light and a buzzer to remind the front occupants that they should "buckle-up" becomes standard on all GM cars.

—GM enters into an agreement to form a joint venture company, General Motors Iran, Ltd. In December 1978, GM exits from both the plant and the country.

—GM enters into a joint venture with Shinjin Motor Company of Seoul, Korea, to build and market cars in Korea. In 1982, Daewoo Group assumes managerial control and renames it Daewoo Motor Company, Ltd. GM retains a 50% stake until 1992.

* * *

1973

—GM manufactures the first production car equipped with an air cushion restraint system as an option.

—GM and the UAW agree to establish the National Committee to improve the Quality of Work Life.

—The Arab oil embargo and ensuing gasoline price increases lead to a rapid and unexpected rise in sales of small Japanese-built cars in the U.S.

* * *

1974

—GM introduces the catalytic converter, a technology it developed in the 1960s. All 1975 model cars sold in the U.S. and Canada are equipped with these catalytic converters to comply with provisions of the Federal Clean Air Act.

—GM proceeds with plans for an unprecedented downsizing of its U.S. cars.

* * *

1975

—Chevrolet introduces the Chevette in October. This U.S.-built "T-car" was first designed by Opel and is also manufactured by GM subsidiaries in Argentine, Brazil, and England and sold under the names Kadett, Chevette, Gemini, and K-180.

In the case of GM, we see a move to change with consumer needs for efficiency and convenience and federal demands for safety and environmental protection. The loss of market share due to Japanese imports rallied GM to become pro-active.

What we glean from the timeline view above is GM's responsive governance and willingness to act "in time." If we then choose significant data from GM's annual financial reports from 1975 to 1990, what we see corresponds favorably to the ongoing decisions the company made. This is why understanding a company's annual report is so crucial. Beyond the broader brush strokes, the report reveals—for the smart reader—a specific view of just how well the company is really doing. Chapters 4 and 5 offer a section-by-section analysis for easy reference. Looking at the long view of a company will help you make the best investment decision.

We turn now to a company that since its inception in 1901 has continued to dominate the beverage industry, essentially on the back of only one product—Coca-Cola. Where Philip Morris and General Motors used diversification to ride economic waves, Coca-Cola, for the most part, has used singular product focus to sustain profitability.

After the low-calorie TAB experiment took off, attention was re-focused on keeping Coke #1 with the comeback slogan "It's the Real Thing." Once again branding, trademark, and marketing kept Coke in the forefront and in front of the American public. The famous hour-glass-shaped Coca-Cola bottle was finally granted registration as a trademark in 1977.

The '70s spewed forth new slogans and ads seemingly on an annual basis. They included "I'd like to buy the world a Coke" (1971); "Coke adds Life" (1976); and the "Have a Coke and a Smile" ad with "Mean" Joe Greene all refreshed with a sense of well-being and "All's Well With the World" when you have a Coke.

The '80s brought some unusual events for the company. In 1982, Diet Coke was introduced to consumers. The difference between Diet Coke and TAB marked the first-time use of the Coke trademark on a product other than Coca-Cola itself. And, of course, the surprise of all time was the "new" Coke incident of 1985. Hoping to circumvent its slipping market share, the company changed its formula and launched the "New Coke" in 1985. However, when consumers soundly rejected it, the company listened. The original recipe was brought back as "Coca-Cola Classic" two months later. Not looking back for long, the company also launched Cherry Coke.

By the time America marched into the '70s, "It's the Real Thing" had made a dramatic comeback. From bottled Coca-Cola for our troops in 1941, to widely available metal cans in 1960, Coke had used intrinsic diversification to serve a thirsty public. In 1971 when young people from around the world gathered on an Italian hilltop to sing "I'd like to buy the world a Coke," Coca-Cola launched itself into a global position. In 1986, the Company's 100th anniversary, two large U.S. bottlers combined to form Coca-Cola Enterprises. Coca-Cola is now the best known, most admired trademark in the world.

Once more, we see how Coca-Cola appraised and analyzed the American economy over a 100-year span. Today, despite numerous contenders over the past 50 years, Coca-Cola is still "Number One."

Perhaps most dramatic of all the eras featured, the '70s and '80s stand out because of the technological advances. Most of us remember or have seen "2001: A Space Odyssey" with its renegade computer HAL (a transposed acronym for IBM). The original computer inhabited an entire room in 1968. By 1971, Intel had created the first single-chip, general purpose microprocessor that IBM utilized for commercial and consumer use. This revolutionized an industry in which changes would be made and abandoned month-by-month. As an investor, how do you handle a speeded-up environment? How do you view a company within such a time-intense landscape?

A revolution in technology was afoot and only the best minds would be able to drive their corporations to continuing success. Between 1972 and 1979, the following technological milestones would take place.

THE HISTORY OF INTEL

At the heart of the Information Age, we look back on a short history filled with innovation and industry-leading technology. The development of this revolutionary company is a story of vision, willingness to embrace change, and just plain luck.

Life Before the Microprocessor

The microprocessor has changed our lives in so many ways that it is difficult to recall how different things were before its invention. In the 1960s, computers were filled with vacuum tubes. Their expensive processing power was available only to a select few in government labs, research universities, and large corporations. The mid-1960s development of the integrated circuit (co-invented by Intel founder Bob Noyce) had enabled the miniaturization of electronic circuitry onto a single silicon chip, but skepticism filled the air: the large-scale integration of transistors onto silicon was still an emerging business.

At its founding in 1968, Intel's unique challenge was to make semiconductor memory practical. This was a stretch, considering that silicon memory was at least 100 times more expensive than magnetic core memory, the leading technology at the time. But Intel's founders felt that semiconductor memory's advantages—a smaller size, greater performance, reduced energy consumption—would convince manufacturers to try the new technology. Success started modestly, when a Japanese manufacturer asked Intel to design a set of chips for a family of high-performance programmable calculators. At the time, all *logic* chips (which perform calculations and execute programs, as opposed to *memory* chips, which store instructions and data) were custom-designed for each customer's product, a process limiting the widespread application of any one logic chip.

That was all about to change. The original Japanese calculator design called for at least 12 custom chips. But Intel engineer Ted Hoff rejected the unwieldy proposal and instead designed a single-chip, general-purpose logic device that retrieved its application instructions from semiconductor memory. As the core of a four-chip set, this central processing unit not only met the Japanese company's calculator needs but also could be plugged into a variety of applications without needing to be redesigned.

IBM

When IBM celebrated its 20th anniversary of the PC (August 19, 2001), on hand to celebrate were the heads of Microsoft and Intel, who benefited greatly from IBM's success. Though we view IBM as the father of personal computing because of its standing in the industry, it wasn't the first to market. Apple was already selling some 10,000 to 20,000 Apple IIs monthly. Others were also promoting desktop computing. "But IBM gave it the air of legitimacy," says International Data Corp. analyst Roger Kay. Turned out in less than one year, the original IBM PC utilized a 4.77 megahertz Intel processor with 16 kilobytes of memory and Microsoft DOS 1.1 software.

Sealed hard disks (often called Winchester disks) took their place as the primary data storage medium, initially in mainframes, then in minicomputers, and finally in personal computers starting with the IBM PC/XT in 1983.

Before Apple and IBM burst onto the personal computing scene, the CP/M was developed by Gary Kildall in 1974. This particular operating system, though, was bypassed by PC manufacturers and CP/M fell away.

The First Personal Computer—MITS Altair

Although the Altair wasn't actually the first personal computer, it was the first to grab attention. Two thousand of them were sold in 1975—

more than any computer before it. Costing only $439, the Altair was a build-it-yourself kit based on Intel's 8-bit 8080 processor and included 256 bytes of memory (expandable to a few Kb), a set of toggle switches, and an LED panel. If you wanted a keyboard, screen, or storage device you had to buy expansion cards! For 4 and 8 Kb Altairs, MITSD offered a BASIC interpreter. This interpreter was the first product developed by Bill Gates's and Paul Allen's new company, Microsoft.

The Commodore PET

The PET was the beginning of a line of low-cost Commodore computers that brought computing to the masses. Like the Apple II, the PET ran on the MOS 6502, but the PET cost only $795 compared to Apple's $1,298. It included 4 Kb of RAM, monochrome graphics, and used an audio cassette drive for data storage. It also included a version of BASIC in ROM. The keyboard, cassette drive, and small monochrome display all fit within the same trapezoidal one-piece unit.

The Radio Shack TRS-80

Still in 1977, the TRS-80 (lovingly called the Trash-80) was the third of the first three consumer-ready personal computers. The base unit was essentially a thick keyboard. Although it had some following, the TRS-80 was soundly defeated in the marketplace by the Apple II, and later by the Commodore 64.

By 1981, Intel's microprocessor family had grown, attracting 2,500 design wins in a single year—an unprecedented figure. Among these was a company looking for parts for its first PC—IBM. Intel's long-term commitment to the microprocessor product line, along with its ability to manufacture in volume, was proof enough for IBM to choose the 8088 as the "brains" of its first PC. IBM jumped out in front of everyone else. Could it maintain that position?

John R. Opel's appointment as CEO in 1981 saw the IBM brand entering homes, small businesses, and schools. The narrower applications of the '70s became mainstreamed in the '80s. John F. Akers's CEO appointment in 1985 saw IBM streamlining operations and re-deploying resources. IBM began to realize that the once popular "Selectric" typewriter did not represent the future of technology. The typewriter division was sold to another firm and the proceeds and workforce used to further PC development. Still, the 1980s were a difficult time for IBM as well. The PC revolution put computers directly in the hands of millions of people and with sales forecast at an initial 250,000 units for a five-year period, IBM was overwhelmed when the first month's sales surpassed that figure. Also, having been a business-to-business company and not having dealt on the retailer/consumer level before propelled IBM into "quick learn" and survival mode. IBM was in a serious place of re-invention: by 1993, it would experience net losses that would reach nearly $8 billion.

Investors during this period would have to re-evaluate their current or future holdings. We know today that IBM regained its footing and is secure in its position as a giant. How, then, can an investor analyze a company for investment purposes when revolution from without threatens the company within? Companies with management teams that can shift with the needs of the consumer base by adapting new technologies and forging alliances to bring diversification and new products can outlast those threats.

THE GROWTH OF WAL-MART

In the midst of these technological developments, a new kind of retail giant was born. Sam Walton spent the late '60s opening variety stores in Arkansas and Missouri. Looking forward to the next decade, Walton first allowed his company's stock to be traded publicly in 1970, and then introduced his "profit-sharing" plan to Wal-Mart employees to improve their income. In addition, stock options and store discounts were offered—benefits that are commonplace today, but Walton was one of the first to implement them.

In 1977, Wal-Mart made its first of many acquisitions: 16 Mohr-Value stores in Michigan and Illinois. In 1978, Hucheson Shoe Company was acquired. Pharmacy, auto service center, and jewelry divisions were also introduced in this year. By 1983, U.S. Woolco stores were also part of the Wal-Mart empire. In 1990, Western Merchandisers, Inc., of Amarillo, Texas, was acquired, along with McLane Company of Temple, Texas, and in this year Wal-Mart became the nation's number one retailer. In 1993, Pace Warehouse clubs were added, along with 122 Woolco stores in Canada in 1994. In 1998, Wal-Mart acquired 21 Werkauf units in Germany, adding 74 Interspar units in Germany in 1999.

Walton developed Wal-Mart's unique decentralized distribution system, which created the edge needed to further growth in the 1980s amidst growing complaints that the "superstore" was squelching smaller, traditional "Mom and Pop" stores. In 1983, "people-greeters" were implemented, adding a personal touch to all the stores. Also, in 1993, the first one-hour photo lab opened at the Tulsa, Oklahoma, store.

Wal-Mart opened its first international store in Mexico City in 1991, followed by another in Puerto Rico in 1992. In 1993, the company formed Wal-Mart International Division. By 1997, Wal-Mart was the number one employer in the United States, with 680,000 associates and 115,000 international associates. This was also the year that Wal-Mart replaced Woolworth on the DJIA. When Sam Walton died in 1992, he was the world's second richest man, behind Bill Gates.

As an investor, when researching a company, you must view it in its landscape; in other words, you must research the entire business sector and industry as well. What may look like a company anomaly may, in fact, be an industry-wide phenomenon and vice versa. That is why investing for the long-term also means investing in the top companies within an industry.

CHAPTER FIFTEEN

The 1990s into the New Millennium

The '90s were truly the high tech age. The World Wide Web debuted in 1992 and even the giants had to re-evaluate how they did business. In 1994, 3 million people were online. The estimate for 2003: well over 1 billion cruising the Informational Highway.

Technology wasn't the only challenge facing big business and investors. Mergers dominated this decade with companies—some old and venerable—being swallowed and re-organized on what seemed like a daily basis. This was also the decade of violence, sex scandals, terrorism, school shootings, health care crises, social security controversies, and a booming economy. Americans were consuming like never before in the booming economy as unemployment reached an all-time low.

The millennium arrived without incident and concern over the technological ramifications of Y2K became a quickly outdated cliche. The year 2000 saw dot.coms boom then bust (not unlike the tech boom in 1968). The NASDAQ became a war zone and the casualties high. The terrorist attack of 2001 closed the stock markets for four days and they reopened to what many anticipated to be a sell-off day. Despite economic fears, economists and market analysts held to their convictions of the market stabilizing. To get a better sense of how the market reacted to and rebounded from major historical events, see Table 15.1.

Looking at the broader, historical view, we see that prior to the '90s, the United States moved toward a more service and information

TABLE 15.1   Dow Jones Market Reactions to Significant Events

Event	Date of event	Initial % market gain/loss	% change after 22 days	% change after 6 months
Fall of France	May 9–June 22, 1940	-17.1	-0.5	7.0
Pearl Harbor	Dec. 6–10, 1941	-6.5	3.8	-9.6
Truman upset victory	Nov. 2–10,1948	-4.9	1.6	1.9
Korean War	June 23–July 13, 1950	-12.0	9.1	19.2
Eisenhower heart attack	Sept. 23–26, 1955	-6.5	0.0	11.7
Sputnik	Oct. 3–22,1957	-9.9	5.5	7.2
Cuban Missile Crisis	Oct. 19–27, 1962	1.1	12.1	24.2
JFK assassination	Nov. 21–22, 1963	-2.9	7.2	15.1
U.S. bombs Cambodia	Apr. 29–May 26, 1970	-14.4	9.9	20.7
Kent State shootings	May 4–14, 1970	-4.2	0.4	13.5
Arab oil embargo	Oct. 18–Dec. 5, 1973	-17.9	9.3	7.2
Nixon resigns	Aug. 9–29, 1974	-15.5	-7.9	12.5
USSR in Afghanistan	Dec. 24, 1979–Jan. 3, 1980	-2.2	6.7	6.8
Hunt silver crisis	Feb. 13–Mar. 27, 1980	-15.9	6.7	25.8
U.S. bombs Libya	April 15–21, 1986	2.6	-4.3	-1.0
Financial Panic '87	Oct. 2–19, 1987	-34.2	11.5	15.0

Panama Invasion	Dec. 15–20, 1989	-1.9	-2.7	8.0
Gulf War	Dec. 24, 1990–Jan. 16, 1991	-4.3	17.0	18.7
Gorbachev coup	Aug. 16–19, 1991	-2.4	4.4	11.3
ERM U.K. currency crisis	Sept. 14–Oct. 16, 1991	-6.0	0.6	9.2
World Trade Center bombing	Feb. 26–27, 1993	-0.5	2.4	8.5
Russia/Mexico Orange Cty	Oct. 11–Dec. 20, 1994	-2.8	2.7	20.7
Oklahoma City bombing	Apr. 19–20, 1995	0.6	3.9	12.9
Asian stock market crisis	Oct. 7–27, 1997	-12.4	8.8	25.0
U.S. Embassy bombings—Africa	Aug. 7–10, 1998	-0.3	-11.2	6.5
Russian LTCM crisis	Aug. 18–Oct. 8, 1998	-11.3	15.1	33.7
Averages		**-7.1**	**3.8**	**12.5**

Source: Information in this chart was gathered by Ned Davis Research Group.

processing economy. Certain manufacturing sectors like iron, steel, autos, rubber, and textiles began to decline. With auto imports on the rise, this sector in particular began to shrink, adding to the unemployment rate.

Service industries continued to grow. Still, there was a disparity between highly paid workers (like technicians, engineers, etc. in computer-related positions) and low-paying custodial, retail, and fast food positions.

A strong global economy also impacted business relationships. Major American companies have roots in globalization that go back as far as the late 19th century. In the 1950s, we saw one of the first great pushes toward opening European facilities. Again in the '70s a wave of globalization rose, driven largely by the U.S. and Japan. The '90s saw computers and the Internet linking businesses worldwide as never before. Money and words could be transmitted instantly without government intervention.

The end of the century saw a complete global economy; Americans numbering in the millions were linked tightly to this network. Some companies chose foreign soils for their physical operations in order to cut costs and maximize profits. This of course meant job losses for some Americans; however, foreign money was invested here in reciprocity—especially in banks, real estate, and brick-and-mortar ventures. Indiana and Tennessee, for example, became locations for auto production by Japanese manufacturers. While this global economy produced significant profits, a rising trade deficit became an unfortunate by-product as Americans bought more foreign products in contrast to those sold abroad. America's financial markets also became linked causally to world events. A good example of this occurred in the Fall of 1998 when issues in Japan, Europe, and elsewhere caused the homefront market to fibrillate.

This was a time for nations to collaborate and offer regulatory organizations. In East Asia, APEC (Asia Pacific Economic Cooperation) joined America and several Asian countries. The 1988 NAFTA agreement (North American Free Trade Agreement) between the United States and Canada was expanded in 1994 to include Mexico. In that same year, GATT (General Agreement on Tariffs and Trades) was signed by the U.S., thus lowering trade barriers and creating a dispute-solving arm known as the World Trade Organization (WTO).

The early '90s also saw corporate layoffs numbering in the hundreds of thousands. The term "downsizing" became a staple of the corporate lexicon, and was considered essential for viable competition in the world economy. The numbers of part-time and temporary workers grew, stripped of benefits or prospects for advancement. Fortunately, the end of the '90s saw a shrinking federal deficit, lower unemployment numbers, and general prosperity.

Organized labor was not immune to global economic impact. Loss of blue-collar jobs meant a drop in union memberships. Unions began to lose their lobbying edge in politics. President Reagan's unilateral solution to the air controllers' strike in 1981 sent a clear message that continued through the '90s. Income disparities between management and factory workers also widened—by the mid '90s, every dollar earned by an average worker was matched by several hundred dollars paid to a CEO.

Labor's lost power became management's gain. To counter the soaring costs of company-paid insurance, for example, HMO's (Health Maintenance Organizations) offered financial respite for hard-pressed corporate budgets. By the end of the '90s, 60% of the American population was enrolled. With this dramatic shift came controversy. A line was drawn between advocates of the HMO who touted its preventative approach toward dealing with illness and adversaries who decried the loss of doctors' discretionary power, a lack of choice of doctor for patients, and an overall sacrifice to the fiscal bottom line. America in 1999 was experiencing a very different economy, even from that of the '80s.

Let's look at five of our giants and see where they stand in the new millennial economy. We'll begin with Johnson & Johnson, a company whose future looks healthy and that offers investors strong investment potential.

Never one to balk at change, Johnson & Johnson jumped into the '90s by forming the first biotech company ever to function as a subsidiary of the parent health care company. JNJ also acquired other companies in areas where growth was desired—McNeil Laboratories in 1959, the division of McNeil into two companies in 1977 (one of which developed and produced Tylenol), and in 1993 a third McNeil company, Ortho-McNeil Pharmaceutical. Later in 1995, JNJ and Merck Consumer Pharmaceuticals produced a joint venture whose shining star was Pepcid AC—the first such advancement for heartburn in over a hundred years.

JNJ also expanded their skin care business by acquiring RoC, S.A., (France) in 1993. 1994 saw the addition of Neutrogena Corporation, followed by AVEENO in 1999. Both of these additions reflected a high-end move to capture a more sophisticated market.

Beauty aside, the scope of clinical diagnosis was broadened when JNJ acquired Kodak's Clinical Diagnostics in 1994. Their Ortho Diagnostics Systems and Clinical Diagnostics combined in 1997 to form Ortho-Clinical Diagnostics. Other advancements in cardiology, circulatory disease, and urology were linked to other mergers and acquisitions during the "snatch and grab" nineties.

In 1997, with breast cancer an issue of strong national and international concern, JNJ acquired Biopsys Medical, Inc., and then quickly merged into Ethicon Endo-Surgery, Gynecare, and FemRX—all of which produced diagnostic and treatment devices for a broad spectrum of female disorders and diseases.

The acquisition of DePuy, Inc., in 1998 marked a major strategic coup for JNJ. At $43.7 billion cash, this was JNJ's largest acquisition ever. The result was an even better orthopedics company, which soon became a leading player on the world stage. Overall, between 1989 and 1999, JNJ acquired 45 companies and divested itself of 18 that were no longer viable.

One should also note that JNJ continues to pour substantial monies into research and development, along with special licensing arrangements. Johnson & Johnson continues, in the broadest sense of the term, to be competitive. Whether creating new companies or acquiring existing ones, JNJ keeps a sharp eye both to its present and to its future.

Having expanded worldwide, JNJ has international affiliates in more than 50 countries, including Australia, Sweden, Japan, Greece, Korea, and Australia. The company has also established new markets in both the People's Republic of China and Eastern Europe. Foremost, perhaps, among these moves was the joint venture of JNJ Limited and Shanghai Johnson, which still produces BAND-AID brand adhesive bandages. Other forays onto foreign soil have taken the company to Moscow, Hungary, Poland, the former Yugoslavia, and the Czech Republic.

The steady growth of JNJ over the years has been directed by five successive board chairmen. As we approach 2003, JNJ encompasses a family of 190 companies whose products are found in more than 175 countries.

The company's more than 99,000 employees are engaged in producing products that serve a broad segment of medical needs. They range from baby care, first aid and hospital products to prescription pharmaceuticals, diagnostics, and products that are related to family planning, dermatology, and feminine hygiene.

Johnson & Johnson is the world's most comprehensive and broadly based manufacturer of health care products, as well as a provider of related services for the consumer, pharmaceutical, and professional markets.

Another giant, General Motors, is also in the driver's seat when compared to the competition.

Sensing that automobile manufacturers would fare better by banding together, William Durant took a dying Buick Motors (1904) and transformed it into General Motors Company in Flint, Michigan, in 1908. In total, he had bought 17 companies by 1910. In 1915, his meeting with race car driver Louis Chevrolet produced another company, followed by a score of others over the years—Frigidaire, Hyatt Roller Bearing, Opel, and others. By 1927, it was the industry leader, a position it has held onto ever since and despite economic setbacks.

After wartime munitions production (WWII) and pollution-control responsiveness during the '70s, GM joined the '90s with mergers and acquisitions—Isuzu, Fuji Heavy Industries, Hughes Electronic, Primestar, and the commercial finance unit of the Bank of New York.

Although it was decided to officially terminate the Oldsmobile brand in 2001, GM strives to be the drive-master with winners on diverse tracks, including the reinstatement of the retro name "Impala."

McDonald's and the Big Mac are winners in their own field— retail fast food. Despite operating in a culture and economy obsessed with optimal health, their processed food continues to rake in big profits.

Although the company started as a Midwestern, grassroots operation, by 1990 the Big Mac and all its buddies had made it all the way to Moscow. In the same year, McDonald's Corporation offered full disclosure on its ingredients by posting complete nutritional profiles in all of their restaurants. *Life* magazine responded by making founder Ray Krok one of the "100 Most Important Americans of the 20th Century."

McDonald's stock continues to be number one among the most widely held, popular stocks for both individuals and investment clubs. In 1993, *Money* magazine praised McDonald's for being the favorite stock of the 30 in the Dow Jones Industrial Average. Its previous placement on both the American Stock Exchange and the Chicago Stock Exchange (both major market indexes) had occurred in 1991.

The mid-nineties saw McDonald's expand its worldwide presence—the world's largest restaurant is in Beijing and is two stories high, has 28,000 square feet, seats well over 700, and employs 1,000. Even a kosher McDonald's opened its doors in Israel in 1995.

Following the movement of other "giants" into mergers and acquisitions during the '90s, McDonald's in 1996 signed a 10-year contract with the Walt Disney Company. This merger made McDonald's Disney's dominant promotional partner in the food industry and extended marketing rights to more than 100 countries. McDonald's thus became linked to Disney theatrical releases, theme parks, and videos.

A man of vision, Ray Kroc turned the McDonald Brothers little burger stand into the food and licensing giant we now know.

"Coke Adds Life"—the campaign slogan of Coca-Cola in 1976 says it all. The company is still the beverage leader. Whether utilizing sports celebrities like "Mean" Joe Greene of the Pittsburgh Steelers to endorse their product or creating the "World of Coca Cola" in Atlanta, Georgia, Coca-Cola chooses marketing venues that root the company firmly in consumer soil. Ongoing sponsorship of both Summer and Winter Olympics added further prestige to the company's image. What Coca-Cola has done to create and maintain its "giant" status is to quench two thirsts—the physical and the cultural. Coke is America; America drinks Coke.

American Express is one of the financial and service giants with a rich and diverse history. From an employee meeting in 2000 came this statement from American Express Chairman and CEO Harvey Golub: "For a company—any company—to survive for 150 years is staggering. Only a handful of our colleagues in the Fortune 500 are even close: Levi Strauss, Coca-Cola, Procter & Gamble. For a company to not just survive over that time period—but to prosper—is to surmount incredible odds. But American Express has done just that." As a result of the Trade Tower bombings of September 11, 2001, American Express has had to move its facilities from the World Financial Center to continue its work.

Begun as a freight company (1850) and moving into the financial arena with money orders (1882) and the invention of the Travelers Cheque (1891) we are still familiar with today, American Express has had a colorful past.

By 1895, American Express had established the first exclusive overseas office in Paris and established a foreign currency and exchange bureau two years later. At about the same time Amex was aiding stranded tourists in Europe because of World War I, it began its travel service. But, by 1918 the government commandeered all railroad and express businesses for the war effort. American Express equipment and real estate holdings comprised some 40 percent and the company was put out of the express business. Its other businesses, money orders, travelers cheques, currency exchange and travel bureau helped see American Express through these transformative times and even thrive. Continued growth outside the United States was now inevitable and necessary.

IN 1920, King Constantine and Queen Sophie of Greece, who were living in exile in Switzerland, were recalled to the throne. American Express was called upon to arrange transportation for the royal family and their household goods back to Athens. Impressed with the service, the king granted a banking license to the company. American Express remained the only American company in Greece for 25 years.[1]

The '20s were booming times for American Express, but were no less interesting. By early 1929, it decided to sell off its sluggish American Railway Express business and improve its cash position, only to see corporate raiders finalize the buying of stock positions in the

---

[1]From *Becoming American Express: 150 Years of Reinvention and Customer Service* by Reed Massengill, copyright 2000, American Express Company, New York.

company and take it over in 1929. American Express was now owned by Chase National Bank, so when the market crashed, American Express fared much better than most other companies. By 1933, with the Glass-Steagall Act prohibiting U.S. banks from engaging in non-banking businesses, Chase was forced to spin off American Express stock into the Amerex Holding Company. Because the holding company owned virtually all of the American Express stock and there wasn't enough in circulation, American Express was de-listed from the New York Stock Exchange by 1939.

With the onset of World War II, American Express began to pare down. Two-thirds of its European offices were closed and staff was reduced to help save money. They also helped with evacuations overseas. Fears that the war would end travel and the need for travelers cheques were quickly alleviated when military families moving throughout the U.S. used the service and overseas military began to carry travelers cheques instead of cash. In the beginning of 1944, American Express had only 11 shareholders and some 1,500 employees and 50 offices. By 1950, post-war prosperity brought the company back to 5,500 employees and 173 offices in time for its 100th anniversary.

AMERICAN EXPRESS launched a mission in the mid 1940s called "Operation Pooch" to help stray dogs adopted by soldiers reunite with their masters back in the States. They were responsible for the care and shipment of some 10,000 dogs.

The 1950s were a time for American Express to reinforce its position in the world of travel services and this was greatly reinforced by *Time* magazine's profile of AMEX President Ralph Reed in April 1956. But maintaining profitability would only come with increasing travel or increasing demand for travelers cheques. But continued growth in these areas was difficult. So, in 1958, American Express launched its very first credit card, transforming the company forever. By 1963, the company computerized to handle its burgeoning card business, launched its upscale "Gold Card" in 1968, and bought the Fireman's

Fund American Insurance Companies in 1969. The '70s insured the company's continual growth with high-profile advertising and its own travel magazine. Through acquisitions during the 70's and 80's, American Express diversified its holdings to become a "financial supermarket." In 1977, American Express stock was listed on the New York Stock Exchange.

As the American Express Company continued its commitment to growth in the financial services arena, it never wavered from its original willingness to help when needed, whether it was aiding in the Saigon airlift in 1975, raising funds to restore the Statue of Liberty in 1983, or supporting the World Monuments Watch in 1999.

Finally we come to the "giant" of technology, IBM, still poised to be a giant in the new millennium.

The remarkable story of IBM parallels its success with Intel. Some historical perspective is appropriate here. When in 1981 Intel's two premier chips—the 16-bit 8086 and the 8-bit 8088 processors—captured 2500 design wins, it was IBM that incorporated the new technology in what would become the first PC, or personal computer. When Intel introduced a more powerful chip in 1982, it was IBM who housed it in the PC-AT. 1985 brought an even bigger and better chip to the table and the Compaq Desk Pro was constructed.

As new and more powerful chips appeared from Intel, IBM matched product to physics. The Pentium Processor, which debuted in 1993, set a new benchmark for power and speed. The computer market had now proliferated into three groups: enthusiast/professional, performance, and basic PC. Within each of these groups, IBM secured a viable niche.

In its first 30 years, Intel technology has enabled developments that were unimaginable a quarter century ago, and IBM has walked hand in hand with this giant-twin. We may be even more amazed at what emerges over the next 30 years. As microprocessors become faster and more powerful, an endless array of new applications will develop and existing applications will spread to the far corners of the world. We will witness further integration of audio, video, and conferencing capabilities with the aid of the Internet. At home, more and more people will be able to view and print family photos from their digital camera, using an intuitive photo editing program to remove red-eye, lighten dark backgrounds, and incorporate the photos into family newsletters and Web pages.

The increase in computing power will also be used to make computers easier to use. Voice and handwriting recognition, local control of complex Internet-based applications, and lifelike animation demand considerable computing power—all available in the Intel microprocessor road map.

IBM has paced technology to implement those products best suited to a wide array of consumers. Such vision will likely keep IBM in the forefront of "giant" successes as the millennium progresses.

Now that we've walked with the giants and learned the reasons for their ongoing success, let's summarize their commonalities. Armed with these, the investor can be an informed, savvy consumer—able to look incisively at annual reports, timelines, and historical context. The characteristics and strategies shared by successful companies are:

Adaptability

Alliances

Diversification

Management maneuverability

Media responsiveness

Vision

The first of these is adaptability, that ability of a company to re-think and reshape its structure and functionality in the face of both external and internal changes. Alliances with others help create diversification and diversified interests means growth. Management readiness to move swiftly in the face of diversity to protect consumers or its good name reflects a company working as a team. And, a management team that looks to the future can create endless possibilities for a company. As investors, there is a lesson to be learned from good, solid tried-and-true companies: we must be flexible, responsive, and look to the future.

Investing Resources

EDUCATIONAL ORGANIZATIONS

American Association of Individual Investors (AAII)—Offers basic and enhanced memberships. Benefits include subscription to *AAII Journal*, research portfolios, and other publications. Advanced memberships include *Computerized Investing* magazine, website, and guides. AAII also hosts local chapter events. *www.aaii.com*.

National Association of Investors Corporation (NAIC)—Offers individual and investment club memberships, as well as computer group and youth memberships that provide educational resources. NAIC supports regional chapters and hosts investor fairs. Members receive a subscription to *Better Investing* magazine (see Magazines and Websites below).

RESOURCE PUBLICATIONS

How To Invest In Common Stocks: The Complete Guide to Using The Value Line Investment Survey. Value Line Publishing, Inc., 220 East 42nd St., New York, NY 10017-5891. 1-800-634-3583; email: *vlcr@valueline.com*; *www.valueline.com*.

Stock Market Encyclopedia. Published quarterly by Standard & Poor's, with full-page reports for each S&P 500 stock. *www.standardandpoors.com*. 1-800-438-2000.

MAGAZINES

Barron's—Weekly business and financial magazine published by Dow Jones & Company. *www.barronsmag.com*. 1-800-369-2834.

Business Week—Weekly business magazine focusing on personal business, the economy, and finance. P.O. Box 53235, Boulder, CO 80322-3235. *www.businessweek.com*. 1-800-635-1200.

Better Investing—Magazine of the National Association of Investors Corporation (NAIC). P.O Box 220, Royal Oak, MI 48068. *www.better-investing.org*. 1-877-ASK-NAIC.

The Economist. 111 West 57th St., New York, NY 10019. *www.economist.com*. 212-541-5730.

Forbes. 28 West 23rd Street, 11th Floor, New York, NY 10010. *www.forbes.com*. 212-366-8999.

Fortune. 1271 Avenue of the Americas, 15th Floor, New York, NY 10020. *www.fortune.com*. 1-800-621-8000.

Money. Time & Life Building, Rockefeller Center, New York, NY 10020-1393. *www.money.com*. 1-800-633-9970.

NEWSPAPERS

The New York Times. Comprehensive business section, published weekdays and Sunday. *www.nytimes.com*. 1-800-NYTIMES.

The Wall Street Journal. Business and investment coverage, published daily by Dow Jones & Co. *www.wsj.com*. 1-800-369-2834.

Investors Business Daily. Market quotes and statistical information along with news stores. *www.investors.com*.

WEB SITES

www.better-investing.org—The online version of the NAIC's magazine (see Magazines, above).

www.bloomberg.com—Financial services, news and media company.

www.bostonstock.com—The Boston Stock Exchange

www.bullmarket.com—Features financial investing newsletters available via e-mail, an investing service, and financial news and education.

www.buyandhold.com—An online broker service geared toward long-term investors.

www.cftech.com—Includes updated and historical listing of the Dow Jones Industrial averages and Standard & Poor's 500 index.

www.cnnfn.com—CNN Financial Network's website.

www.daytrading.about.com—Features a day trading resource guide.

www.dlbabson.com—David L. Babson & Company, Inc., a large investment counseling firm.

www.dowjones.com—Information on the Dow Jones Industrial Average, published by the *Wall Street Journal*. See also *www.djindexes.com* and *www.indexes.dowjones.com*.

www.e-analytics.com—Equity Analytics, Ltd., a quantitative and statistical research firm.

www.economist.com—See Magazines, above.

www.fool.com—The Motley Fool, multimedia financial education company.

www.hoovers.com—Hoover's Business Network, offering financial information geared toward businesspeople, with capsule profiles of various companies.

www.individualinvestor.com—News and commentary site for the individual investor.

www.industryweek.com—Online version of *Industry Week* news magazine.

www.invest-faq.com—The Investment FAQ, general educational site regarding investments and personal finance.

www.investopedia.com—Includes investment terms dictionary, articles, and e-mail tutorials.

www.learninvesting.com—Educational site for beginning investors.

www.money.com—Online version of *Money* magazine.

www.moneycentral.msn.com—Microsoft and CNBC Network financial news site.

www.moneypages.com—The Syndicate, an investment news and education website.

www.morningstar.com—Features portfolio tracking, investment information, and other tools.

www.nasdaq.com—Information and tracking site for the NASDAQ stock market. See also *www.nasdaqfunds.com* and *www.nasdaqnews.com*.

www.nytimes.com—Online version of *The New York Times*.

www.phlx.com—Website for the Philadelphia Stock Exchange.

www.stockz.com—Includes short- and long-term stock picks for site members, and research and information for non-subscribers.

www.sustainability-index.com—Dow Jones Sustainability Group Index. Provides indexes to benchmark performance of investments in sustainability companies and funds.

www.tdwaterhouse.com—Website for global financial services firm.

www.thestreet.com—Provides market tracking, financial news, and analysis.

www.upside.com—*Upside Magazine* online offers personalized e-mail newsletters to its members.

www.valueline.com—Some information is free, however, access to the quarterly sheets is not. See website for fees. The Value Line Survey is a resource at most public libraries.

Annual Reports— Letters to Shareholders through the Decades

The Procter & Gamble Company
1959 **Annual Report**

Letter to Shareholders

To the shareholders of
The Procter & Gamble Company:

We submit herewith the annual report of The Procter & Gamble Companies for the fiscal year ended June 30, 1959.

FISCAL YEAR RESULTS

Consolidated net sales of all the Companies for the year were $1,368,532,426. This compares with net sales for the preceding year of $1,295,163,269.

Consolidated net earnings for the fiscal year ended June 30, 1959 amounted to $81,697,965, with the comparable figure for the preceding year being $73,196,618. Earnings per share on the average number of shares of common stock outstanding during the year were $3.96 as compared with $3.56 for the prior year.

Dividends of $2.10 per share were paid on the common stock during the fiscal year ended June 30, 1959. This compares with dividends of $2.00 per share in the preceding year. So far in the fiscal year beginning July 1, 1959 a quarterly dividend of $.55 per share has been declared and is payable August 15.

During the past year consolidated working capital was increased and long-term debt was reduced. This further strengthening of the financial position of the Companies is very gratifying.

The fiscal year ended June 30, 1959 was the largest year in Procter & Gamble's 122-year history. Both in this country and overseas the business went forward in a sound and healthy way. Many of our long-established brands showed real vitality and, of course, the strength of these older brands makes up the foundation on which we build. In addition, during the year the Company introduced several new products which are progressing in a satisfactory manner.

A CONSTANTLY CHANGING BUSINESS

Our business is never static. It is in continuous evolution to meet the many and rapid changes in consumer needs and desires. Older products must constantly be improved and new products must frequently be introduced in order to maintain our position in the vigorously competitive fields in which we operate. The fact that over 70% of our household volume today is in products that weren't even in existence at the close of World War II is evidence of the rapidly changing nature of our business.

STRENGTH OF ORGANIZATION

In this rapidly changing picture, Procter & Gamble's ability to compete successfully year after year depends to an overwhelming degree on the strength of the Company's organization. It depends on the ability and character of the men and women who work for the Company. The task of developing people and of building and improving the organization is a never-ending one. It receives closer attention than any other single phase of the Company's activities and properly so. During the past year we feel the Procter & Gamble organization—like its sales and profit picture—continued to improve.

In order to provide work space for our growing organization in the research and technical branch of the business, we completed this past spring the construction of the new Winton Hill Technical Center. This new technical center will supplement the Technical Center at Ivorydale and the Miami Valley Laboratories, all of which are in nearby but different locations within the Cincinnati area. The Company's continued ability to offer improved products to the consumer depends to a great degree on research and development work, and the new Winton Hill facilities should help our people to progress with this important activity.

NEW PRODUCTS

The constantly changing nature of the business is evident in many ways.

For example, a trend toward the liquid form of washing products, begun in previous years, continued during 1958–59. This trend is especially noticeable in products for washing dishes and for general household cleaning purposes. In line with this trend, during the past year the Company introduced nationally Ivory Liquid detergent for dishwashing and for laundering fine fabrics. For general cleaning purposes, the Company also introduced broadly a new liquid product called Mr. Clean.

The trend toward increased use of toilet bars containing synthetic detergent continued during 1958–59 but at a slower rate than in the previous two years. In Zest, Procter & Gamble has one of the leading products in this field.

In the fall of 1958 the Company completed national introduction of Jif—a peanut spread which competes with peanut butter and other spreads. Also during the past year our new Duncan Hines cake mixes were introduced into more than half of the United States. The area in which we are selling Duncan Hines cake mix products has thus been extended to virtually the entire country. In addition, other types of

Duncan Hines baking mixes are being sold in certain sections of the country. The consumer acceptance of the Duncan Hines prepared baking mixes in all areas where they are being sold is encouraging.

New products are also being developed in the Toilet Goods and Paper Products Divisions. In Toilet Goods, for example, in addition to our line of toothpastes, shampoos and home permanent waves, we introduced Secret Deodorant in part of the country this year. In Paper Products we are marketing White Cloud bathroom tissue in experimental areas as a supplement to our line of Charmin paper products. We look forward to the further growth of these divisions of the business.

In December 1958 the Company sold four of its soybean crushing mills in the United States. The sale of these mills was desirable because of the changes which had taken place in the availability of soybean oil and in the marketing of soybean meal in this country. We continue to operate cottonseed crushing mills in the United States and a soybean crushing mill in Canada, and our business in these crushing facilities during the past year was satisfactory.

CELLULOSE PULP BUSINESS

The Company operates plants for the production of dissolving cellulose pulp at Memphis, Tennessee and Foley, Florida. Cottonseed linters are used as the raw material at Memphis; Southern pine and hardwoods are used as the raw material at Foley.

The volume of business shipped from the Memphis plant in 1958–59 increased substantially over the previous fiscal year. The present prospect is that there will be a large increase in the cotton crop during the current growing season. This should result in a further improvement in the volume of business at this plant.

In December 1958 we completed the second expansion of the wood pulp plant at Foley. Although we have not yet developed a volume of business large enough to utilize the full expanded capacity of this plant, we were able to increase our volume of wood pulp products during the past year.

OVERSEAS OPERATIONS

Good progress also has been made in Overseas operations during 1958-59. During the year we established broad operations in Italy for the first time. Tide, Camay, and Spic and Span were introduced throughout Italy and we believe there is a good opportunity for our products in that country. During the year we also completed a second plant in Canada and we currently are building a detergent plant in Morocco.

We recently announced plans to sell our Cuban assets other than our international trademarks. This will not represent a complete withdrawal from the Cuban market, since the purchasers will continue to produce and market products using brand names under license from us.

We now have an important volume of production and major marketing operations in eight countries outside the United States. These are Canada, Great Britain, France, Belgium, Italy, the Philippines, Mexico and Venezuela. In many of these countries, new brands have been introduced successfully during the past year. Our products are also being marketed in 118 other countries, primarily through export channels although in some instances through production from small local plants.

PENDING LITIGATION

In last year's letter we mentioned the Federal Trade Commission's proceeding against our Company attacking its acquisition of the Clorox business. Presentations have been made to the Hearing Examiner appointed by the Federal Trade Commission and at the date of this report we are awaiting his decision. The proceedings to date have not altered the basis of the original complaint: that Procter & Gamble is successful in its present fields, has gained broad acceptance for its products among housewives and other consumers, and that this kind of competence may result in some restraint of competition in the bleach business. We do not believe the evidence proved the charge, and we repeat our last year's statement: we cannot believe that the Federal Trade Commission as a judicial body will find any legal or factual basis for this proceeding.

It is also necessary to remind you again that the Company along with certain other defendants in the soap industry faces the Department of Justice's antitrust suit. This is the suit which was filed in December 1952, was dismissed by the New Jersey Federal District Court in September 1956 before it came to trial, and was, in effect, reinstated by the Supreme Court in June 1958. The Company is currently preparing for the trial of this case. We remain confident of our ability to prove in court that the soap industry has been and continues to be one of the most competitive in the country and that the charges of restraint of competition and monopoly are baseless.

The financial statements showing the consolidated financial position of the Companies as of June 30, 1959 and the results of their operations for the year, together with figures for the prior year, are set forth in the following pages.

Our more than 61,000 shareholders, we believe, can join the management in looking forward to the year ahead with considerable confidence. The wide diversification of the Company's products and its well-trained organization, together with an expected high level of industrial activity in the foreseeable future, give us good reason to expect the continued sound development of the business.

Respectfully,

Chairman of the Board

Cincinnati, Ohio
August 7, 1959

President

The Procter & Gamble Company
1967 Annual Report

To Our Shareholders:

FISCAL YEAR RESULTS

We submit herewith the annual report of The Procter & Gamble Company for the fiscal year 1966–67, which ended June 30, 1967.

Net sales for the year were $2,438,746,000, an increase of 9 percent over net sales of $2,243,177,000 for the previous year.

Net earnings amounted to $174,110,000, an increase of 17 percent over net earnings of $149,447,000 for the preceding year.

Net earnings per share on the average number of common shares outstanding during the year were $4.08. Net earnings per share for the previous year were $3.47.

Dividends of $2.10 per share were paid during the fiscal year. The amount paid the preceding year was $1.92½. The present quarterly dividend is at the rate of $2.20 yearly.

The Company's volume on consumer products increased at a faster rate than on industrial products. Some of our less profitable bulk business actually declined. This contributed to an increase in earnings that was greater than the increase in sales.

Overall, it was a good year for Procter & Gamble. Sales, earnings, and dividends each advanced to a new high.

LONGER-TERM RESULTS

Although these results of the past fiscal year are satisfactory, we again wish to emphasize—as we did in our last annual report—that we regard the results of any one year as being of limited significance. It is the long-term record that counts and the past fiscal year represents merely the latest step in the continuing growth of Procter & Gamble.

The record of the Company's growth between 1957 and 1967 is shown on page 16 of this report. As you can see, the $174,110,000 earnings in the fiscal year just ended compares to $67,800,000 earnings a decade ago.

You can also see from this record that our rate of advance from year to year has been uneven. Nevertheless, the Company's earnings have gone ahead every year and the cumulative increase over the ten-year period has been significant.

In this ten-year period, there has been very little effect of inflation in our selling prices. For example, the average prices of our U.S. packaged soap and detergent brands are slightly lower today than they were ten years ago. The same statement can be made about our U.S. shortening and oil prices. There have been both advances and declines in the prices of our products during this ten-year period, but overall we believe our record of price stability has been outstanding.

At the same time, constant product improvement has been our objective. Every product in our line has been improved in value and performance many times during this past decade.

CLOROX DECISION

This record of the Company's progress has been accompanied during the past fiscal year by certain unfavorable events.

One of these was the Supreme Court's decision in the Clorox case. In our annual reports for each of the past nine years we have told you of the ups and downs of the Clorox antitrust litigation. On April 11, 1967, the Supreme Court reversed the unanimous decision of the Court of Appeals and ruled that Procter & Gamble must divest itself of the Clorox business.

We are moving with dispatch to implement the Supreme Court's decision. One of our most experienced Vice Presidents has been relieved of all his other responsibilities in order to devote full time to supervising this task, which is a difficult and time-consuming one. The Clorox business represents an asset of substantial value, and it will be our aim to convert it into a new and different asset of comparable value and then to use this new asset for the benefit of the Company's shareholders. We believe that the Clorox divestiture can be accomplished without any major interruption in the Company's future progress.

FOLGER CONSENT DECREE

Another disadvantageous development during the past year had to do with the Federal Trade Commission's consent decree in regard to our Folger coffee business.

Under this decree Procter & Gamble retains and continues to operate the Folger coffee business. However, we must sell our Houston plant and operate the business under certain restrictions for the next five years. Of course, the sale of the Houston plant will be arranged so as not to interfere with our ability to supply Folger products to our customers.

As everyone knows, the coffee business in the United States is highly competitive and we dislike not being able to compete on a fully equal basis with the other major companies in this field. Also, the sale of our Houston plant will be disruptive to our business and the new plant which we must construct to take its place will be costly. Nevertheless, we expect our Folger business to continue to move ahead. Procter & Gamble is in the coffee business to stay—and to grow.

As part of the Folger consent decree, Procter & Gamble also agreed not to purchase any more grocery product businesses in the United States in the next seven years without the prior approval of the Federal Trade Commission.

LIMITATION ON FUTURE ACQUISITIONS

We agreed to this limitation on our business for two reasons:

First, it seemed to us to be a relatively small price to pay to avoid another long period of litigation with the Federal Trade Commission. It also seemed to us to be the most important thing we could do to remove one possible source of future disputes with the Commission.

Secondly, the purchase of new businesses has not played a large part in Procter & Gamble's growth. Quite overwhelmingly, the Company has grown as a result of its own creativity—by creating new products, by creating new performance values in its existing products, and by creating new markets and new opportunities within its established markets.

The record of the past two years is a case in point. The 31% increase in earnings during these two years was accomplished without any acquisitions at all in the United States and with only one very small acquisition abroad (the Rei-Werke company in Germany, which was reported to you in our last annual report).

CAPITAL EXPENDITURES

The Company is currently engaged in the largest construction program in its history. The largest part of this new construction program is to provide additional capacity for our growing business and for the improvements in our products which will make this growth possible. It also provides for extensive new research and development facilities.

ORGANIZATION

During the past fiscal year there were a number of changes in the organization of the Company.

Mr. Donald H. Robinson, A Vice President-Group Executive and Director, retired after 37 years of dedicated and productive service to the Company.

Mr. Edward G. Harness, Vice President-Group Executive, was elected a Director of the Company to fill the vacancy on the Board caused by Mr. Robinson's retirement.

Mr. John W. Hanley was elected Vice President-Group Executive.

In addition, the following men became Vice Presidents of the Company:

Mr. Richard S. Runnels was elected Vice President-Finance.

Mr. John G. Smale was elected Vice President-Toilet Goods Division.

In this letter to our shareholders we have included the key figures showing the Company's progress, a brief recital of some of the events of the past year, and a listing of some of the organization changes. Unfortunately, in a letter of this kind, it is impossible to convey adequately what we regard as the real story of the Company's progress.

The real story now, as always, is the growing strength of the Company's organization. Practically all Procter & Gamble employees join the Company right out of school and develop their special abilities within the business. The finding of young men and women with high and diverse talents, their training, their rapid development to positions of responsibility—this is the most important and exciting story of the Company. It is the primary source of our strength and the one that provides the greatest assurance to our shareholders for the future.

In reporting on the record results of this past fiscal year, we think it is important to acknowledge the Company's reliance on, and indebtedness to, its many dedicated employees at all levels of the business who are responsible for these results.

Respectfully,

Chairman of the Board

Cincinnati, Ohio
August 4, 1967

President

The Procter & Gamble Company
1973 Annual Report

To Our Shareholders

FISCAL YEAR RESULTS

We submit herewith the annual report of The Procter & Gamble Company for the 1972–73 fiscal year which ended June 30, 1973.

Net sales for the year amounted to $3,906,744,000, an increase of 11% over net sales of $3,514,438,000 for the previous year.

Net earnings amounted to $302,103,000, an increase of 9% over net earnings of $276,310,000 for the preceding year.

Earnings per share were $3.68, which compares with $3.38 for the previous year.

Dividends of $1.56 per share were paid during the fiscal year. The equivalent amount for the previous year was $1.50. The quarterly dividend was increased to an annual rate of $1.80 in July, 1973. The amount of the increase in both 1972 and 1973 has been within Federal Government guidelines.

The above results indicate that Procter & Gamble had another good year. Our sales approaches the 4 billion dollar mark. Our earnings topped $300,000,000 for the first time. For the seventeenth consecutive year, our sales, earnings per share, and dividend payments have established new records.

DEVALUATION OF THE DOLLAR

Several unusual factors affected our earnings during the past year. The devaluation of the dollar, the rapid rise in our raw material costs, government price controls, and the phosphate issue all had an impact on our business.

As a result of the devaluation of the dollar, our assets outside the United States have been revalued upward to the extent of $10,300,000. Normally, this all would have been taken into profits. Instead, $5,000,000 of this amount has been used to double our reserve for foreign operations. With floating currencies, we feel this action is appropriate and that the new total of our reserve is adequate under the circumstances. The remainder or $5,300,000 is included in the earnings of our International business.

RISING COSTS AND PRICE CONTROLS

As the result of rapidly rising raw material costs and price controls which prevented our ability to cover these costs, our U.S. earnings were considerably below what they would otherwise have been.

We are, for example, a major user of agricultural products. Our cost of tallow, coconut oil, soybean oil and cottonseed oil all rose between 50% and 100% between January and June, 1973. Our cost of green coffee, wood pulp, peanuts, flour, potatoes, and other agricultural products which we buy in quantity also rose during the fiscal year. This upward movement in our raw material costs took place under price controls—including Phase II, Phase III, and the freeze following Phase III. Under price controls we were not able to recover our increased costs in higher prices for our own products. This had a substantial negative effect on our earnings during the fiscal year which ended on June 30.

It should be noted that Phase IV, which was announced just a few weeks ago on July 18, will not relieve the pressure on our earnings. The exact rules and regulations of this program have not yet been published as this letter goes to press and, of course, the exact cost as well as the availability of our raw materials cannot yet be ascertained. However, it now looks as if—at least for the next month or two—the unfavorable impact on our U.S. earnings could be magnified rather than diminished under this latest version of price controls.

We have three basic viewpoints about price controls in general, based on our experience with them in other parts of the world as well as in this country:

First of all, we do not think they are good for the economy. We do not think that over any period of time they result in lower prices to consumers. Frequently they result in higher rather than lower prices and thus work in a negative way. One of the worst things about them is that once a country adopts price controls, it is difficult to let go of them.

Secondly, we expect Procter & Gamble to get along under price controls at least as well as any other company in the various industries in which we operate.

Thirdly, we keep our minds on our long-term objectives of building the business and the organization. We do not believe that price controls can last very long in an economy as complex as ours in the United States and they will not divert us from our long-range goals.

PHOSPHATE ISSUE

The phosphate issue also affected our earnings. At various times during the fiscal year we were out of business on packaged laundry detergents in Chicago, Buffalo, Miami and the state of Indiana. We are now back in business in Chicago as the result of a Federal Court decision declaring the local law there to be illegal. We are back in business in the other areas as the result of new discoveries in our research laboratories which enabled us to develop non-phosphate detergents which are safe for use in the home and which we believe are superior to other non-phosphate products in washing clothes.

Nevertheless, the non-phosphate granulated products on the market today—our own included—are not as effective in washing clothes as phosphate detergents are. For this reason, we shall continue our efforts to present the facts on this complex problem to legislators, the public and to the courts in an effort to bring about a change in laws which force housewives to use inferior washing products when there is no detectable benefit to the environment. We regard that as our obligation to consumers.

At the same time we are continuing our effort to reduce the phosphate content of detergents. It is indeed a major effort. Through June 30 of this year we have spent a total of $130,000,000 to accomplish this objective. As a result of this effort, and barring unforeseen events, we expect that by the end of next year the phosphate content of most of our detergents in most areas of the country will have been cut in half without reducing their effectiveness. Beyond that, we hope to be able to make further reductions in phosphate levels as soon as we can do so without sacrificing either their safety or efficacy. We shall continue our effort to do this even though we remain convinced that the elimination of phosphates from detergents alone will not benefit the nation's waterways. The true road to better water quality in this country is through better sewage disposal systems which effectively eliminate all nutrients from urban waste.

In spite of these problems, our earnings in the United States went forward. Our volume, stated in both units and dollars, moved ahead in every U.S. household products division and in our industrial business. Our overall business in the United States is strong and growing.

INTERNATIONAL

This year our earnings outside the United States amounted to $88,589,000. This is more than double what they were just three years ago.

Practically all of our established businesses abroad are going forward. In addition, during the past fiscal year, we moved into several new areas. We introduced Pampers in Canada, Crest toothpaste in Venezuela, and Head & Shoulders shampoo in England. We started test markets on Crest toothpaste in England and on Pampers in Germany. Our new joint venture in Japan officially began to do business in January, 1973. In addition, in Canada our new pulp plant in Grande Prairie, Alberta is starting production this month.

Our business abroad should continue to progress. Indeed, the opportunities for Procter & Gamble products overseas seem almost unlimited.

LONG-TERM GROWTH

Every year for the past several years we have stressed in our Annual Report that our Company takes the long view in the development of its business and does not regard the results of any one year as being particularly meaningful. We constantly position the Company for the long-term future as opposed to immediate gains in sales or earnings.

The results of this thinking are shown in our past record and, once again, we want to refer you to the record of the past fifteen years. It is shown on page 19 of this report. In the fifteen years since 1957–58, our earnings per share have increased at an average rate of 9.9% per year compounded. This means that our earnings per share have more than quadrupled in the last fifteen years. At the same time, we should point out that the growth in our earnings per share from one year to another during this period has varied widely—from a low of 2% to a high of 19%. The fluctuations by quarters, of course, are even greater and even less meaningful. It is the long-term record that counts. We think the long-term record indicates that our business has grown in a satisfactory manner.

Much of an annual report of this kind is necessarily concerned with the material progress of the Company. However, financial reports do not tell the whole story by any means. The growth of our organization is perhaps even more important but it is difficult to convey the way it is developing in a report to shareholders. Some of the changes in the top management group are listed on page 7 but they don't tell the full story either. Suffice it to say that, at all levels, we believe our organization is constantly growing in strength.

The way the Company carries its social responsibilities is equally important. Here, too, the story is difficult to convey adequately in an annual report. One aspect of this responsibility we have tried to cover fully. It concerns the way we handle our forest lands and this is presented on page 8 of this report. It is illustrative of the fact that in this area also, we are planning for the long-range future.

NEIL McELROY

All of us in Procter & Gamble were saddened by the death of Neil McElroy on November 30, 1972.

He joined Procter & Gamble in 1925 and rose to become President and Chief Executive Officer in 1948. He served in that role for nine years until 1957, when President Eisenhower called on him to be Secretary of Defense. He returned to the Company to serve as Chairman of the Board from 1959 to 1971 and then as Chairman of the Executive Committee of the Board of Directors until a month before he died.

He made many great contributions to his company, his community, and his country throughout his distinguished career. He received honors too numerous to mention. But most of all he was a warm personal friend of all of us, and we miss him very much indeed.

* * * * * * * * * * * *

As we look to the new year, we recognize that severe problems face us in the many countries in which we do business. Inflation and monetary problems are almost universal. Where they exist, governmental controls and protectionist trade policies often warp and inhibit genuine economic growth.

However, Procter & Gamble has faced far more uncertain and adverse conditions in the past. Through wars, depressions, and revolutions in many different areas of the world, we have been able to survive and to build steadily. In the light of our past performance, we cannot feel dismayed about the problems facing us today—particularly in view of the Company's resources and the momentum of its business at the present time. Our greatest resource of course, is the organization of men and women who make up The Procter & Gamble Company. It is chiefly because of them that we can look forward to many more years of growth and progress.

Respectfully,

Howard Morgens

Chairman of the Board

Edward G. Harness

President

August 6, 1973
Cincinnati, Ohio

The Procter & Gamble Company
1983 Annual Report

FINANCIAL HIGHLIGHTS

We submit herewith the Annual Report of The Procter & Gamble Company for the 1983 fiscal year which ended June 30, 1983.

Net sales for the year amounted to $12.5 billion, an increase of 4% over net sales of $12.0 billion for the previous year. The increase in unit volume was greater than the increase in dollar sales.

Net earnings amounted to $866 million, an increase of 11% over net earnings of $777 million for the preceding year. Earnings per share were $5.22, which compares with $4.69 for the previous year. These per share figures have been adjusted for the two-for-one stock split which was effective January 21, 1983.

Dividends of $2.25 per share on the new share basis were paid during the year. The comparable amount for the previous year was $2.05 per share. The current quarterly dividend rate is $2.40 per share on an annual basis.

New records were established for sales, unit volumes, and earnings. Dividend payments increased for the twenty-seventh consecutive fiscal year.

In total, we are reasonably pleased with our progress this past year. It was gratifying to see unit volume growth in the United States and in our International business despite depressed levels of economic activity in virtually all of the countries where we do business.

UNITED STATES BUSINESS

Domestic net earnings totaled $758 million which represents an 11% increase over the previous year. Unit volume growth was broadly based, with each of the U.S. consumer product divisions establishing new shipment records. Margins continued to show improvement, with cost savings and productivity gains major contributing factors. During the past few years, selling prices in our domestic consumer products business have increased in aggregate at rates well below the comparable rates of general inflation. This past year, we generally held the line on prices, marking the smallest rate of increase during the past decade.

Efforts increased during the year to broaden our product base through the development of new brands. We are particularly encouraged by generally strong consumer acceptance of several new brands currently in test markets. If these positive trends continue, we expect that overall investment in new brand activities will be significantly higher in the coming year than last year.

During the past year, Duncan Hines Creamy Frosting, a convenient, ready-to-spread topping for Duncan Hines cakes and other home-baked products, was expanded to national distribution. Head & Chest, an over-the-counter cold medicine, was also introduced nationally. In recent months, we have substantially broadened the distribution of Banner, a new bathroom tissue, into most of the United States east of the Rocky Mountains.

In June, the Company purchased a privately-held, soft drink bottling company with plants in Lexington and Louisville, Kentucky. This acquisition is a logical step in the further development of our experience in the soft drink business. Also acquired during the past year was the Tender Leaf Tea brand which, while in limited distribution, provides an initial learning opportunity in a growing category of the beverage business.

Industrial and institutional unit volume was up over the previous year but continuing pressure on selling prices in some categories, especially wood pulp, had an adverse effect on earnings. Continued gradual economic recovery in the industrial sector of the U.S. economy should lead to a further improvement in volume and increased profitability in the coming year for the Company's industrial business.

INTERNATIONAL OPERATIONS

Net earnings from international operations amounted to $105 million, an increase of 19% over last year. Good progress was made during the past year in both unit volume growth and earnings despite continuing economic recession in many countries and general weakening of foreign currencies in relation to the U.S. dollar. The currency impact was particularly significant in Mexico and Venezuela.

In Europe, new volume records were established in each of the major countries. Market shares were healthy with notable gains in the packaged detergent and disposable diaper categories. New brands which were expanded nationally during the past several years continued to contribute importantly to the growth in volume and market share. During the past year, new brands expanded to national distribution included Ariel low suds laundry detergent in Italy, Bounce dryer-added fabric softener in the United Kingdom and Switzerland, Zest bar soap in the United Kingdom, Vizir heavy-duty liquid laundry detergent in Belgium and Holland, and Fairy light-duty liquid detergent in Spain.

Elsewhere, improved margins were achieved in Canada, the Philippines and the Middle East, together with increases in both unit volume and market share.

CAPITAL EXPENDITURES

Capital expenditures totaled $604 million, or less than the $650 million average level for the three previous years. Almost 40% of this past year's expenditures were directed towards cost saving projects as an integral part of the Company-wide program to reduce costs and to improve productivity. Projects to increase capacity and to improve product quality constituted the bulk of the remaining expenditures. In the coming fiscal year, we are projecting a higher level of capital spending with similar emphasis on capacity, cost savings and quality improvement projects.

PRODUCTIVITY

Capital investments to reduce costs and to improve operating efficiencies are but one part of the Company's ongoing productivity program. The creative efforts of Procter & Gamble employees throughout the world are the key factors responsible for the significant cost savings and productivity gains made in recent years. Beginning on page 9 of this Report is a pictorial essay which illustrates some of their accomplishments. This program is an essential element in helping to combat the effects of inflation in our costs and in keeping the prices of our products competitive in the marketplace.

RESEARCH AND DEVELOPMENT

To meet the changing needs of consumers and to ensure the future growth of the Company we are firmly committed to a broadly based research and development program. This includes basic research with emphasis on new technologies as well as applied research to develop new products and to maintain the vitality of existing products. Last year, $327 million was invested in research and development activities, a 14% increase over the previous year.

LONG-TERM GROWTH THROUGH NEW BRAND INVESTMENT

The foundation of Procter & Gamble's operating philosophy is to manage the business with long-term growth as the primary goal, rather than focusing solely on profit objectives in any single year. The Company's growth record over the past fifteen years is shown on pages 30 and 31 of this Report. The rate of growth for both sales and earnings has varied from year to year. However, during this fifteen year period, earnings per share have increased at an average annual rate of 11%, testimony, we believe, to the long-term health and vitality of the business.

Looking to the future, an essential element in building upon the Company's long-term growth record is the successful development and marketing of new brands. This requires sizable investments in research and development, start up of new manufacturing capacity, and introductory marketing expenditures. Initially, this has a negative effect on earnings. The benefits accrue over later years from a broadened product base, paving the way for future growth.

FINANCIAL STRENGTH

The ability to capitalize on new business opportunities whenever they arise is importantly dependent upon the Company's financial strength in being able to fund the sizable investment required. The Company's balance sheet and financial position continue to be strong. During the past year, our financial liquidity improved with a $362 million increase in cash and marketable securities. A major factor contributing to this improvement was a reduction in working capital investment by our operating divisions.

Long and short-term debt in relation to total capital employed remains relatively modest. During the past few years, the level of debt has not changed significantly as the bulk of cash needs has been met through internally generated funds. This gives the Company considerable flexibility in meeting new brand investment needs as well as the financial requirements for our established business.

THE ECONOMY

Two major economic challenges confront the developed nations of the free world. The first is to generate economic recovery from the world-wide recession. The second is the longer-range objective of sustaining economic recovery without rekindling the fires of inflation. Achievement of both goals will play an important role in providing the foundation for economic prosperity in the years ahead—for individual citizens throughout the free world as well as for businesses including Procter & Gamble.

In the United States most economic indicators are currently favorable. There are beginning signs of a gradual recovery and the rate of inflation is down from the double-digit levels of recent years. On the other hand, federal spending continues to increase to levels that will produce unprecedented federal budgetary deficits in the years ahead. The pressures these deficits exert on interest rates pose a threat to nurturing and sustaining economic recovery and to holding down inflation.

Bipartisan governmental support is urgently needed to control spending and to reduce these deficits. We believe such a unified effort is essential if the United States is to lead the way for all nations into an era of real economic growth.

ORGANIZATION CHANGES

During the past year, the following changes were made in the Board of Directors and senior officers of the Company.

George C. McGhee, former Chairman of the Board of Saturday Review/World, former United States Ambassador to Turkey and Germany, and former Under Secretary of State for Political Affairs, retired as a Director after thirteen years of distinguished service.

Robert A. Hanson, Chairman, President and Chief Executive Officer of Deere & Company, and Theodore F. Brophy, Chairman and Chief Executive Officer, GTE Corporation, were elected to the Board. These actions increased the Board to nineteen members.

Power McHenry was elected Senior Vice President and General Counsel. He was previously Vice President-General Counsel.

* * *

The Company's success in meeting the competitive challenges of past years has been achieved due to the resourcefulness and dedication of the 62,000 Procter & Gamble men and women throughout the world. Their strength provides the greatest assurance to our shareholders of continuing Company progress in the years ahead.

Respectfully,

O.B. Butler

Chairman of the Board

John G. Smale

President and Chief Executive

August 10, 1983

Procter & Gamble
1991 Annual Report

To Our Shareholders

The new decade has already served notice on the business world that we have entered a time of changing expectations. The timeless benchmarks of product performance, convenience and customer service remain paramount and largely unchanged.

But today, consumers everywhere are demanding better value, more consistent quality, greater environmental sensitivity and more substantive information about the products they buy.

Your Company is well positioned to meet these increasingly diverse standards of consumer satisfaction.

Our commitment to Total Quality systems has sharpened our organization's focus on continuous improvement in quality and continuous reduction in costs.

Our proactive environmental policy is positively impacting the way we formulate and package our products, and the way we operate our offices and plants.

Our packaging, advertising and public relations policies are guided by the principle that all communication about our products will always be clear, informative and truthful in impression, as well as in fact.

These policies and principles—and many others traditional to Procter & Gamble's 154 years of successful operation—underlie everything we do.

FISCAL YEAR HIGHLIGHTS

Innovative product initiatives and the globalization of our business continue to represent the leading forces behind the Company's ongoing growth.

Results for the fiscal year ended June 30, 1991, were good. Earnings, sales and dividends again achieved records.

Net earnings grew 11% and earnings per share were up 10%. Worldwide sales registered a 12% gain. Dividends were up $.20 per share to $1.95, marking the 35th consecutive fiscal year of increased dividend payments.

Unit volume growth, particularly in the international business, made the greatest contribution to earnings growth. Favorable currency exchange rates were also a factor.

Our international gains were very strong and broadly based, with all regions up versus a year ago. Business outside the U.S. now represents 46% of total sales, up from 40% last year, reflecting the growing contribution of this business. Our brands are now marketed in more than 140 countries, with on-the-ground operations in 51 countries. Highlights of our business by region follow:

A great year in Europe

The Laundry, Cleaning, Paper and Beverage business in Europe delivered share and earnings growth in most countries and categories. The greatest gains traced to compact product introductions in our two largest categories, diapers and laundry detergents. During the year, good progress was made in our newer geographies, including Portugal and Turkey, and in former East Germany.

Our European Health and Beauty Care business had record volume and profit growth. The business was up in every European country and category. Growth was led by revitalization of some of our strong, but underdeveloped brands, such as Vidal Sassoon. This brand is now Europe's best selling shampoo, following the introduction of Vidal Sassoon Wash & Go two-in-one shampoo and conditioner. Similarly, Oil of Olay has become the best selling facial moisturizer in Europe.

P&G enters Eastern Europe

In June 1991, we established our first business ventures in Eastern Europe. Procter & Gamble was the first foreign company to acquire a major Czechoslovakian business under the new Privatization Law. The company—"Rakona"—is Czechoslovakia's leading supplier of laundry and cleaning products. In Hungary and Poland, we entered joint ventures to market diapers, shampoos, bar soaps and dentifrice.

A Record Year in the Middle East

Thanks to the exceptional commitment of our P&G organization in the Arabian Peninsula, our businesses in the Middle East and Africa exceeded their previous record year volume. This was achieved in spite of losing the Kuwait business for most of the year.

Expansion in Latin America

Good progress has been made in broadening our business base beyond our successful, established laundry and cleaning categories. We experienced healthy volume growth in diapers, feminine protection pads and hair care products in Mexico, Venezuela and Puerto Rico. Our first P&G brands in Brazil—Pert Plus and Pampers—are off to a strong start. In Argentina, our recent joint venture with Eguimad, a leading producer of diapers and feminine pads, will help round out our presence in the southern part of the continent.

Strong momentum in Japan and the Pacific Rim

Japan again delivered outstanding volume and profit growth, due to a substantial improvement in our laundry detergent business and continued share growth on Pampers as well as Whisper feminine pads. We have broken ground on our new research and development center in Osaka Bay and expect the project to be completed in March 1993.

In the Asia/Pacific area, every country but one reached new volume records. We have just started expansion of Ariel laundry detergent in India, thus entering one of the largest detergent markets in the world. Our three-year-old subsidiary in the People's Republic of China has made an excellent start, proving that Chinese consumers have the same interest in buying high quality P&G products as we have experienced in more developed markets such as Hong Kong and Singapore.

A Tough but Productive Year in the U.S.

Despite last year's difficult economic conditions in the U.S., volumes were up modestly. Slower consumer demand in several categories, and a reduction in trade and pantry inventories resulted from the recession's impact. Increased price competition affected profit margins in several of our businesses, particularly wood pulp, where excess world capacity led to sharply lower prices. Also, in the Food & Beverage Sector, results were below expectations.

At the same time, it was a productive year for our U.S. organization, with more new product initiatives reaching the consumer than in any period in recent history. New concentrated powder detergents were expanded from test markets into more than 75% of the country and will soon be sold nationally. A new liquid Tide detergent with bleach-like performance and a new multi-purpose spray cleaner, Cinch (from Spic and Span), are being introduced nationally.

In the Hair Care category, new two-in-one shampoo and conditioner products have been introduced on the Vidal Sassoon and Head & Shoulders brands. Oil of Olay has introduced a new line of foaming facial cleaners and UV-light protection moisturizers. The Health Care sector has expanded a new "neat squeeze," no-mess Crest package and Metamucil has introduced a new wafer product for daily fiber therapy.

Our Paper Sector has introduced all new Pampers and Luvs diaper products designed for different stages of a baby's development, while Always feminine pads has added a line of unique ultra thin products.

In the Food and Beverage Sector, new products have been introduced with special appeal to the increasing diet and health consciousness of consumers everywhere. Two examples being expanded are Simply Jif, a low salt, low sugar peanut butter and an improved Crisco vegetable oil with significantly reduced saturated fat. Our Sunny Delight fruit drink line had a record year of growth and is introducing several new drink items broadly. Foodservice & Lodging Products had an outstanding year despite a slowdown in many segments of the restaurant, lodging and institutional market.

The pace of product innovation on our U.S. business has laid a strong foundation for future growth, and this kind of activity will continue across our business throughout the new fiscal year.

BEAUTY CARE—A WORLDWIDE STRATEGIC VISION

As we look to the future, we see unlimited opportunities for product innovation and globalization of our Beauty Care business. Our goal is to be a world leader in hair care, skin care, cosmetics, sun care, fragrances, personal cleansing and deodorants. We expect these categories to grow in importance as sources of sales and earnings in the years to come.

Within the past three years, we have greatly expanded our hair care and skin care businesses worldwide. About a year ago, we established a significant foothold in men's toiletries and fragrances with the acquisition of Old Spice, and that business is now being integrated and vigorously marketed in all of our geographic regions.

The Company's most significant recent beauty care developments have been in the cosmetics sector, which the Company first entered in 1989 with the merger with Noxell. That business is making excellent progress. We are now expanding Cover Girl cosmetics, the U.S. market leader, in the U.K. Navy, a new women's fragrance developed by Noxell and available nationally in the U.S., is one of the fastest selling fragrances on the market.

International expansion of our cosmetics business has been accelerated by the recent acquisition of the Max Factor and Betrix lines of cosmetics and fragrances from Revlon. Max Factor's key brands include Max Factor cosmetics, the California and Le Jardin fragrance lines, and SK-II, a leading skin treatment brand in Japan. Betrix, based in Germany, is one of Europe's leading cosmetics and fragrances companies. Its major brands include Ellen Betrix cosmetics for women, Henry Betrix toiletries for men and within its Eurocos group, the Laura Biagiotti and Hugo Boss fragrances.

About 80% of the sales of these products occur outside the U.S., thus positioning P&G as a significant worldwide competitor in the $16 billion cosmetics and fragrances market.

ENVIRONMENTAL QUALITY—A PRIORITY COMMITMENT

We are continuing to devote major effort to help find solutions to the world's solid waste problems. Refill packs for many of our brands, including Downy fabric softener in the U.S. and Canada, and our Mr. Clean brands in Europe and Latin America, are reducing packaging materials by about 75%. We have expanded the use of recycled plastic in liquid detergent bottles in the U.S. and Europe.

The Company also is actively involved in helping to establish recycling and municipal composting infrastructures. We have implemented recycling demonstration projects in several localities including Newcastle, England, and Baltimore, Maryland. We have established a $20 million composting infrastructure fund to help inform community leaders about this important new solid waste solution which can help dispose of up to 60% of household waste, including disposable diapers.

Our manufacturing plants worldwide have extensive environmental quality programs. At our Jackson, Tennessee plant, we have reduced overall plant waste by 37% and landfill usage by 79%. In Istanbul, Turkey, two recycling projects have eliminated 10 tons of liquid waste per year. These examples are characteristic of the progress we are striving for at all of the Company's plants.

A STRONGER ORGANIZATION

We have made a number of important system and organization changes to strengthen our competitiveness. We have completed realignment of the U.S. Sales organization to more closely serve our trade customers. We are expanding worldwide use of Customer Business Development Teams to provide substantially better customer service and to lower distribution costs for both P&G and our customers.

This past year we established a new worldwide Regulatory and Clinical Development organization to coordinate all P&G activities involved in securing regulatory approvals for new drugs, cosmetics and other products. This worldwide capability is critical to ensuring that our innovations move quickly to market.

Last month, we created six new operating units and retitled most of the Company's officers. These units better describe the way the Company is organized to manage its business, and they provide increased recognition for additional Company executives.

P&G PEOPLE—THE KEY INGREDIENT

The success of our past years' business traces to the quality of our 94,000 P&G people around the world. Their creativity, energy and dedication enabled the Company to overcome the economic and competitive challenges of the past year and to deliver good results. The excellence of our people is the essence of our confidence that our results will be even stronger in the future.

Respectfully,

Edwin L. Artzt
Chairman of the Board
and Chief Executive

John E. Pepper
President

August 8, 1991

Johnson & Johnson
1944 Annual Report

To the Stockholders of Johnson & Johnson:

During 1944 securities of Johnson & Johnson were offered to the public for the first time since incorporation in 1887. This is the first consolidated annual report published by the Company.

While total sales were slightly less in 1944 than in 1943, sales of products for civilian consumption were substantially greater in 1944 than in 1943. There was little change in net income after taxes.

During the year the Company placed on the market a number of new items: "JOHNSON'S BABY LOTION," Tantalum in sutures and other forms used in surgery, "RAY-TEC" X-rayable sponges, "SULFATHIAZOLE NU-GAUZE STRIPS," "DISPOSIES" diapers, and "BONDEX" mending tape. It developed further markets or improvements in a number of products, particularly "LUMITE" plastic screening, "RAPID-FLO" dairy filters, "STERI-PAD" gauze pads, and the gynecic pharmaceuticals "HEXITAL" and "NUTRI-SAL."

From January 1, 1939 to December 31, 1944 the Company spent large sums for gross capital expenditures for plant, machinery, equipment, and improvements. Its program is not completed and further expenditures are anticipated. The Company recently caused the exchange through a subsidiary of an office building in New York for a textile mill in South Carolina.

The cash position reflects the fact that the Company had bought during 1944 tax certificates to cover all United States income taxes accumulated or owed during the year 1944.

The moderate dividends paid to common stockholders permitted the Company to retire the major portion of its indebtedness. The Board of Directors feels that, in view of the apparently promising opportunities for the investment of further funds in expansion of its production and in view of the increase in sales in the last three years, a conservative dividend policy will be continued until completion of the expansion program is in sight and working capital is adequate. This follows the traditional policy of the Company in paying moderate dividends and thus permitting growth from the Company's own resources without need of outside financing. The Directors envisage continuance of this traditional policy with continued growth.

I express for the Board of Directors and for myself sincere appreciation for the loyalty of the men and women of Johnson & Johnson. Their performance was the significant factor in the development of the Company in 1944, as in all prior years.

ROBERT WOOD JOHNSON,

Chairman, Board of Directors

New Brunswick, N. J.

April 25, 1945

Johnson & Johnson and Domestic Subsidiaries
1951 Annual Report

HIGHLIGHTS of the Year

	1951	*1950*
Sales to customers	$184,661,295	$162,803,153
Net earnings	8,126,460	13,280,798
Per dollar of sales	4.4¢	8.2¢
Per share of common stock	$ 3.78	$ 6.49
Cash dividends—preferred stocks	201,691	348,891
—common stock	2,311,189	3,977,236
Per share of common stock	1.10	2.00
Employees		
Salaries, wages and other employment costs	51,195,678	44,328,525
Number at December 31	11,232	11,224
Taxes—federal, state and local (excluding payroll taxes)	$ 13,959,446	$ 13,050,310
Provision for wear and exhaustion of property, plant and equipment	4,897,174	3,628,074
Additions to property, plant and equipment, less sales proceeds	6,786,946	12,740,512
Working capital	43,676,504	39,777,341
Stockholders' equity	84,008,664	78,469,785
Number of common stockholders	1,946	1,616

To The Stockholders:

In our past annual reports to the stockholders, we have been reluctant to interject "politics." This year we feel that we cannot refrain. The problem has gone beyond partisanship or personalities. Ours is a business country. It either goes forward or recedes. All citizens of whatever party should join in the effort towards re-establishing encouragement for intelligent venture. Only through the creation of such an economic climate can we maintain and improve our standard of living, and at the same time defend ourselves against aggression.

In our business we think it is essential that we face the fact of product obsolescence and for the long-range future provide our highly diversified family of businesses with a steady, though moderate, supply of new opportunities. We believe that such a course contributes to a constantly improving standard of living. However, the extravagance in Government spending and the burden imposed by excessive tax legislation have combined to deny creative business that reasonable opportunity for profit so necessary to planning for new ventures. According to recent surveys, more than half of the present volume of business in drugstores represents products introduced in the past ten years. History will not repeat itself if the present handicaps continue. The public will not be served. The employees' chance for security and advancement will be decreased, and the stockholders' hope for profit will be diminished.

We have long believed that the reinvestment of a considerable portion of earnings after taxes in a few conservative ventures designed to produce new and better products was to the advantage of all concerned. In almost every case, new and better products require new plants and equipment, greater inventories and greater receivables. In the long run, these new and better products improve our service to the public and afford more security and opportunity to both employees and stockholders.

Products, however, do not always succeed and our plans must, therefore, contemplate failure as well as success. The rewards of the successful ventures must be sufficient to absorb the losses on the unsuccessful and to leave an adequate return on the money risked by reinvestment.

The operations of our domestic companies, while producing a substantial increase in dollar sales, showed a decrease in earnings before taxes and a greater decrease in earnings after taxes. Corporate taxes raised to levels higher than in any other country in which we operate have cut deeply into earnings after taxes.

On the other hand, operations of the foreign affiliates in 1951 showed an increase in both sales and earnings after taxes. The increase was sufficient to have justified the reinvestment of past earnings in additional productive facilities.

March 6, 1952   Chairman

Financial Report

EARNINGS

1951 domestic net earnings amounted to $8,126,460 or $3.78 per share on the 2,096,344 shares of common stock outstanding at the year end, compared with $13,280,798 or $6.49 per share on the 1,993,160 shares outstanding at December 31, 1950.

Federal income taxes of $13,155,212 including excess profits taxes of $1,661,600, increased $993,774 over the 1950 total of $12,161,438 which included excess profits taxes of $1,538,000. The tax provision required in 1952 will be still greater, as the higher tax rates will apply to the full twelve months, whereas in 1951 the new rates went into effect on April 1.

The introduction of new and improved products by the Company does not result immediately in large increases in sales and earnings. After a new product is developed and in production, it takes time to create effective national distribution and consumer demand. The Company invested large sums in 1946–1949 for increased facilities, the potential profits from whose production were only partially reflected in its earnings for those years. Greater realization in 1950 and 1951 of the benefits of the Company's large increase in production and sales has been nullified in part by the heavy tax levied on earnings that result not from war-induced stimulation of sales but from the expansion undertaken after World War II.

Reflected also in the lower earnings before taxes in 1951 were the cost of the expanded research staff and facilities, and abnormal costs incurred in establishing new production facilities, particularly at the Dallas plant, which did not reach effective operating levels during the year.

Johnson & Johnson
1961 Annual Report

Two Years in Brief

Domestic Operations

	1961	*1960*
Total Income	$332,185,977	$309,736,985
Net Earnings	16,592,646	15,604,882
Per Share	2.77	2.63
Cash Dividends Paid	5,949,404	5,927,273
Per Share	1.00	1.00
Net Property Additions	15,566,000	17,093,034
Working Capital	82,734,696	79,927,639
Stockholders' Equity	175,411,702	159,912,870
Per Share	29.30	26.95
Number of Stockholders	6,205	5,575
Number of Shares Outstanding at Year-End	5,986,770	5,934,034
Number of Employees at Year-End	15,188	14,616

Worldwide Operations

Total Income	$416,384,015	$386,623,969
Net Earnings	18,255,113	18,727,665
Number of Employees at Year-End	25,466	23,781

Chairman's Report to Stockholders

DOMESTIC OPERATIONS

Earnings and Sales—1961

Consolidated 1961 domestic earnings were $16,592,646, or $2.77 per share, as compared with $15,604,882, or $2.63 per share, for 1960. These figures are based on 5,986,770 shares of common stock of a par value of $5.00 each outstanding at the end of 1961 and 5,934,034 shares outstanding at the end of 1960.

Consolidated domestic sales for 1961 increased by 7.3% to $324,241,772, as compared with $302,046,347 for 1960. The 1961 total sales represent a high in dollar volume for any annual fiscal period in the history of the Company.

Dividends

The Company, during 1961, declared and paid dividends of $1.00 per share on its common stock. Such dividends are reportable by recipients for purposes of United States income tax.

On January 22, 1962, a regular quarterly dividend of $.25 per share was declared payable March 9, 1962, to stockholders of record as of the close of business on February 16, 1962.

Property Expansion and Expenditures

Construction operations began September 1, 1961, on the new Johnson & Johnson surgical dressings plant near Sherman, Texas, which is about 60 miles north of Dallas. The program is scheduled for completion during 1963. The site was purchased in 1960 when the decision was made to move the surgical dressings plant currently located in Dallas to the Sherman area. This transfer is being made because the Company's Texas operations are rapidly outgrowing the Dallas facilities.

During 1961, construction of a new administration building in New Brunswick, New Jersey (see rendering p. 5) commenced on the site occupied for many years by manufacturing facilities which have been moved to other locations outside New Jersey. The new structure will supplement the existing office building on the same grounds and will fulfill a long standing need for additional facilities for management personnel. The building is expected to be ready for occupancy in 1963.

During the year, the new plant of McNeil Laboratories, Incorporated, at Fort Washington, Pennsylvania, was completed, as were additions to the plants of Ortho Pharmaceutical Corporation, Raritan, New Jersey, and Ethicon, Inc., Somerville, New Jersey.

As a result of these and other miscellaneous projects, expenditures for domestic plants and equipment, less cash proceeds, amounted to $15,566,000. The provision for depreciation was $11,402,748. It is anticipated that in 1962 such expenditures for domestic operations will be approximately $17,000,000.

Corporate Organization Changes

Effective January 1, 1962, two new divisions of the parent Company were formed, known as the Robert Wood Johnson Co. and the Johnson & Johnson First Aid Products Division. The Robert Wood Johnson Co., under the direction of Mr. J. E. Burke, handles the marketing of Johnson & Johnson baby products and many of its proprietary drug products. The Johnson & Johnson First Aid Products Division, under Mr. H M Poole, Jr., markets the well-known surgical dressings line. Each has a separate sales-service staff calling on customers nationwide. It has been the traditional aim of the Company to provide the best possible service to our customers. In the light of the continuous growth of the surgical dressings, baby products and proprietary product lines in recent years, it was felt that this aim could best be achieved through the formation of the two new complete and separate marketing divisions, each with a staff of trained sales and merchandising specialists.

Employee Stock Compensation and Options

At year-end, the Company was obligated to deliver over a period of not more than four years 29,189 shares of its common stock in performance of outstanding Stock Compensation Agreements with 902 employees.

At the beginning of the year, 16,151 shares of common stock were issuable pursuant to 37 restricted stock options under the 1952 Restricted Stock Option Plan. Options relating to this Plan were exercised during the year covering a total of 1,745 shares. No options expired or were cancelled. The number of shares issuable pursuant to 35 options outstanding at the close of the year was 14,406. No further options may be granted under the 1952 Plan.

Pursuant to the 1961 Restricted Stock Option Plan, approved at the Annual Meeting of Stockholders held April 11, 1961, options were granted on July 11, 1961, to 144 employees of the Company, covering a total of 139,150 shares of common stock. The options are for a term of ten years but may not be exercised within a two year period following the date they were granted. The option price per share was established as 85% of the fair market value on the date the option is exercised or 85% ($80.00) of the fair market value on the date the option was granted, whichever is the lesser. The market value of the stock on the date of grant was $94.00, as reflected by sales on the New York Stock Exchange. None of these options expired or was cancelled. Since the Plan, as approved, provided for the allotment of a maximum of 300,000 shares of common stock, the number of shares available for allotment under the Plan at the close of the year was 160,850.

Executive Personnel Changes

Effective December 31, 1961, Mr. P. D. L'Hommedieu retired as a Director and member of the Executive Committee of Johnson & Johnson and as Chairman of Foreign Operations after 34 years of service with the Company. Mr. L'Hommedieu joined the Company in 1928 as a Hospital Division salesman, thereafter assuming various executive and management posts, until in 1942 he became Assistant to the President. He was subsequently Chairman of the Board of two of the Company's major affiliates. He has been a member of the Executive Committee of the Company since 1950 and Chairman of Foreign Operations for the past four years. For his lifetime of service and contribution to the welfare of the Company, the management of the Company joins in expressing thanks to Mr. L'Hommedieu.

During 1961, Mr. R. J. Dixson and Mr. C. V. Swank, Directors of the Company, were appointed members of the Executive Committee. Both have key responsibilities in the area of international operations of the Company. Mr. Dixson served as President of Johnson & Johnson International for 5 years, is currently a Vice Chairman of its Board and has been an executive of the Company for many years. Mr. Swank joined the Company in 1936 and served, from 1945 until his appointment to the Executive Committee, as Vice President in charge of Manufacturing. He has been a Director of Johnson & Johnson since 1945 and is currently a Vice Chairman of Johnson & Johnson International.

On January 2, 1962, Mr. A. A. Rohlfing was elected a Director of the Company and appointed a member of the Executive Committee. Mr. Rohlfing joined the Company in 1931, after having been an instructor in engineering at Harvard. He established Cia. Johnson & Johnson do Brasil in 1934 and served as its chief executive officer until his return to the United States in 1959, when he was elected a Vice President of Johnson & Johnson International of which he is now a Vice Chairman of the Board.

INTERNATIONAL OPERATIONS

Sales, Earnings and Dividends

Consolidated net sales of foreign affiliates during the year 1961 were $90,256,062, an increase of 9.6% over the comparable 1960 net sales of $82,321,821. Net earnings in 1961 were $3,290,632 as compared to 1960 net earnings of $4,585,305. Earnings were net of exchange conversion charges of $1,206,691 in 1961 and $385,076 in 1960. These charges in 1961 were due largely to a decline in the value of the Brazilian cruzeiro and, in lesser measure, to declines in the value of the Canadian dollar and the Venezuelan bolivar. In 1960, the charges were due mainly to declines in the value of the Brazilian cruzeiro.

Earnings for 1961 were adversely affected by active competitive factors in some areas, economic instability in others, and losses on certain recently established operations.

Dividends remitted to the parent Company in 1961 were the highest in the history of the Company at $1,628,165 as compared to $1,462,522 in 1960.

Expansion

During 1961, the Company purchased Laboratoria Pharmaceutica Dr. C. Janssen N. V. in Beerse and Turnhout, Belgium, and Research Laboratorium Dr. C. Janssen N. V., in Beerse, Belgium (see illustration p. 7), together with two Janssen affiliates in Holland and West Germany. The Janssen operation has been in the pharmaceutical business in Belgium since 1934, and, during the last four years, it has engaged in an intensive pharmaceutical research program. Janssen maintains its own marketing operations in Belgium, Holland and Germany. This acquisition is expected to broaden Johnson & Johnson's position in the ethical pharmaceutical field.

Expenditures for plant and equipment in all foreign operations were $6,629,000, and it is anticipated that capital expenditures in 1962 will be approximately $5,500,000.

Organization Changes

Commencing in 1962, the method of overall supervision of the International Operations of the Company was changed to follow a pattern of direct line rather than staff management. Several members of the Executive Committee will each be responsible for a major segment of the Company's worldwide activities. This pattern will bring the management of the Company's International Operations more in line with that employed for many years with respect to its Domestic Operations.

On December 30, 1961, Mr. J. F. Brooke retired as Chairman of the Board of Johnson & Johnson (Gt. Britain) Limited. He played the leading role for almost 20 years in the success of the Company's British operations. This company served not only the British Isles, but much of the British Empire and many overseas countries. On behalf of the Company, congratulations and thanks are extended to Mr. Brooke for a job well done.

* * *

On behalf of all directors and officers, I am pleased to express sincere recognition and appreciation of the efforts of our employees, both in the United States and overseas, for their continued loyalty and fine performance.

New Brunswick, N. J.   Chairman of the Board
March 2, 1962

Johnson & Johnson
1976 Annual Report

Chairman's Report to Stockholders

The year 1976 was one of significant accomplishment for the Johnson & Johnson Family of Companies.

Consolidated sales were $2,522,510,000, exceeding sales of $2,224,680,000 in 1975 by 13.4%. Consolidated net earnings were $205,376,000, an increase of 11.7% over earnings of $183,818,000 in 1975. This is the first time our profits surpassed $200 million, which is twice what they were in 1971.

Domestic sales and profit increases were outstanding. We were highly satisfied with the operating performance of our international companies, but their sales and profits were adversely impacted by the effect of currency translations into U.S. dollars.

While we are pleased to report record sales and earnings, we are, as a management, more interested in how effectively the business was strengthened and prepared for the future.

In this regard, it is noteworthy that almost all of our major product franchises around the world either held or gained in share of market during 1976.

At the same time, our companies continue to show the ability to sow the seeds of growth with the introduction of a number of important new products. This is true of all major segments of our business.

We, as a corporation, are also continuing the practice of establishing new companies around the world when our evaluation persuades us there is a reasonable opportunity to build a successful enterprise. One might question this policy in the light of current fluctuations of foreign currencies, but experience has convinced us that the stockholders' best interests are served if we make our decisions based on the long-term opportunity rather than upon short-term considerations.

The most important key to our future growth is, of course, the strength, stability and continuity of our management at all levels of the business.

During 1976 Mr. Richard B. Sellars recommended to the Board of Directors a realignment of top management responsibilities that would result in a smooth transition in a number of key positions. In taking this action well in advance of his planned retirement date, he followed the example of his two predecessors. As a result, I was privileged to be elected Chairman and Chief Executive Officer in November, and Mr. David R. Clare succeeded me as President and Chairman of the Executive Committee.

We are gratified that Mr. Sellars will continue to be actively involved in the affairs of the Company and will serve as Chairman of the Finance Committee, besides continuing as a member of the Executive Committee.

Mr. Stanley C. Anderson has joined Mr. Sellars in devoting full time to the responsibilities of the Finance Committee. Mr. Anderson's responsibilities were assumed by Mr. Victor J. Dankis, who was elected Vice President-Finance, and appointed a member of the Executive Committee. Mr. Dankis has served as Treasurer since 1974.

Mr. Robert E. Campbell has been elected to the Board and Treasurer of the Company. He was Vice President-Finance for Johnson & Johnson International and before that served as General Controller of Johnson & Johnson. Mr. John J. Heldrich, Vice President, Administration, and a member of the Board since 1971, was named to the Executive Committee and given broader management responsibilities.

Mr. Foster B. Whitlock retired in February of this year as Vice Chairman of the Board after giving 38 years of dedicated service to the Company. Mr. Whitlock joined the Company as a salesman and rose to become chairman of Ortho-Pharmaceutical Corporation and to play a key role in the development of Johnson & Johnson's overseas operations in the past two decades. Mr. Whitlock has earned a particular debt of gratitude for his outstanding achievements, which will continue to benefit this Company for many years to come.

Mr. Henry S. McNeil has chosen not to stand for re-election to the Board of Directors of Johnson & Johnson and will resign his corporate office. Mr. McNeil has served as a member of the Board since 1959, the year McNeil Laboratories, Incorporated, was merged into Johnson & Johnson. He served as president of McNeil Laboratories until 1960, when reasons of health forced his resignation, and he was Assistant to the Chairman of Johnson & Johnson from 1962 to 1973 when he was elected Vice President. He has provided astute counsel over the years, particularly in the pharmaceutical phase of our operations, and we are pleased that he will continue as a director of McNeil Laboratories.

In addition to the aforementioned, we continued our practice of making changes in key management posts around the world, taking into consideration not only the operating needs of the businesses, but also the opportunity to provide important management experience for a number of our most promising executives.

As of the close of 1976 our business was composed of 145 enterprises operating around the world with considerable autonomy. Management control is exercised largely through the Executive Committee, assisted by Vice Chairmen and Vice Presidents of Johnson & Johnson International, each with broad operating experience both at the domestic and international level.

We continue to be convinced of the inherent productivity of this highly decentralized environment.

With this in mind, we have tried in this year's Report to focus attention on the importance of our management and the dynamic way in which it is organized. We have done this by giving you a glimpse of some typical activities in the closing months of 1976.

Our form of organizational structure puts a premium on entrepreneurial skills. Our managers are encouraged to run their own organizations, to seize initiatives, and to select and motivate the people who can get the job done.

This report highlights but a small part of the creative energy of our nearly 58,000 employees who "get the job done" day after day in our companies around the world.

We want to thank all of them for the very commendable results in 1976. More importantly, we want them to know that it is because of them that we have so much confidence in the future.

New Brunswick, N. J.   James E. Burke
March 15, 1977   Chairman of the Board

Johnson & Johnson
1982 Annual Report

Letter to Stockholders

WE BELIEVE THE CONSISTENCY OF OUR OVERALL PERFORMANCE AS A CORPORATION IS DUE TO OUR UNIQUE FORM OF DECEN-TRALIZED MANAGEMENT, OUR ADHERENCE TO THE ETHICAL PRINCIPLES EMBODIED IN OUR CREDO, AND OUR EMPHASIS ON MANAGING THE BUSINESS FOR THE LONG TERM.

This statement provided the central focus for a series of meetings held last June in New York with the presidents and managing directors of our 150 companies from around the world.

We feel the theme of this year's annual report, "An Eventful Year," dramatizes the validity of the principles articulated in that statement.

While the TYLENOL tragedy interrupted the consistency of our earnings growth in 1982, it was an event without precedent both in its impact on your corporation and on the American public.

The financial effect of TYLENOL was obvious from our reported results. The combination of the $100 million cost of the capsule withdrawal and the loss of profit on lost TYLENOL sales caused us to report profits in 1982 of $2.52 per share, or essentially the same as the previous year.

While our earnings increase in 1982 would have been within historic patterns if it were not for the TYLENOL incident, the most important effect of the TYLENOL experience on all of us in Johnson & Johnson was not financial but the dramatic reaffirmation of the philosophies by which we manage our business.

DECENTRALIZATION

It is clear now to all of us that our unique form of decentralization worked for us in three ways. First, our employees at McNeil Consumer Products Company performed under extraordinary stress with unquestioned brilliance. The decisions they made and the speed with which they expedited the reintroduction of TYLENOL capsules were undoubtedly due to the kind of concentrated management attention that created the TYLENOL success in the first place.

At the same time, 13 sister companies of McNeil were mobilized to join in the massive effort to keep our customers in the trade and everyone in the medical professions informed of the basic facts in the TYLENOL situation as they unfolded.

And finally, all of our companies worldwide rallied to increase their dedication to their own businesses, as they quickly understood the need for extra effort when one member of the Family of Companies was threatened.

OUR CREDO

While these companies are highly individualistic in the way in which they pursue their own business opportunities, they all were united during the crisis by the principles expressed in our corporate Credo.*

This document spells out our responsibilities to all of our constituencies: consumers, employees, community, and stockholders. It served to guide all of us during the crisis, when hard decisions had to be made in what were often excruciatingly brief periods of time. Most importantly, all of our employees worldwide were able to watch the process of the TYLENOL withdrawal and subsequent reintroduction in tamper-resistant packaging, confident of the way in which the decisions would be made. There was a great sense of shared price in the knowledge that the Credo was being tested . . . and it worked!

---

*We have printed the Credo on the inside back cover of this annual report for those who are not familiar with it.

LONG-TERM ORIENTATION

Because Johnson & Johnson historically has been managed for the long term, it was easier for all of us to make the costly short-term decisions so necessary to the future of TYLENOL and the long-term strength of the corporation.

While the TYLENOL tragedy dramatized the validity of these management principles, this annual report serves to remind us that it was, indeed, but one event in a year of significant accomplishment in building for the future.

Our companies continued to be highly productive in introducing new products in all segments of our business, at the same time broadening the penetration of products into new markets around the world.

The most tangible evidence of our continuing commitment to the long term is in our mounting investment in research and development. In 1982 we spent $363 million, up from $233 million in 1980, for a 56% increase in two years. We now estimate that only 16 U.S. companies spend more in research and development than we do.

The projects that these dollars support represent an increasing commitment to new science and technology that presages an exciting future for all of us.

We strengthened our commitment to new technologies like Nuclear Magnetic Resonance at Technicare. We broadened our exciting relationship with the Scripps Clinic and Research Foundation, where we are working on projects such as the synthetic vaccine program. We also established a new research center in Cambridge, Massachusetts, where a number of new projects are being pursued by our Ortho Diagnostics company. We also continued to take minority positions in new biotechnology enterprises that appear to have promise.

Johnson & Johnson has never been in a better position to work closely with the research community in gaining new insights in the creation of important new business opportunities.

MANAGEMENT

Our organization continues to be refined to take advantage of these developments. We created a new office of external research. Dr.

Ronald J. Brenner heads that function with the explicit task of coordinating the relationship between the Johnson & Johnson Family of Companies and external biotechnology research activities such as the one at the Scripps Clinic and Research Foundation. A physical manifestation of that increased involvement was the creation of the Johnson & Johnson Biotechnology Center, Inc., in La Jolla, California, near Scripps.

In other important management changes, Mr. David E. Collins became a member of the Executive Committee, with management responsibility for McNeil Consumer Products Company, as well as a number of companies in Latin America.

We were also pleased to add two new members to our Board of Directors in 1982. Mr. Paul J. Rizzo, the recently named Vice Chairman of IBM, joined our Board in October 1982, as did Mr. John C. Walcott, a member of our Executive Committee responsible for Johnson & Johnson Products, Inc. and several other operating companies here and abroad.

To summarize, 1982 was indeed an eventful year. Despite the enormity of the TYLENOL tragedy, we are impressed that our value system at Johnson & Johnson survived the challenge placed against it and served society well.

The public was served well because of the extraordinary cooperation that occurred among all the responsible elements of society. The regulatory agencies, the wholesale and retail parts of the distribution system; the various medical professions; the local, state, and federal law enforcement agencies . . . all worked together with the media to alert the public to the danger and to protect them in the process. It is well to remember that two unused bottles of poisoned TYLENOL were recovered as a result of the withdrawal, so lives may have been saved.

We also would like to thank you, our stockholders. Your faith and confidence in us was remarkable, as evidenced by the value of our shares and the numerous letters of support for our TYLENOL activities without a single letter of criticism.

And finally we would like to thank our employees—past and present. Their cooperation and unwavering support provided strength for all of us throughout the ordeal. We all learned during this experience that the reputation of Johnson & Johnson, which had been built carefully for over ninety years, provided a reservoir of goodwill among the public, the trade, the medical professions, the law enforcement and regulatory agencies, and the media, which was of incalculable value in helping to restore the brand.

This reputation was built by our employees. It is because of their continued dedication that we are so confident about the future.

The importance of our corporate Credo was dramatized once again this month when we decided to temporarily withdraw our ZOMAX (zomepirac sodium) prescription analgesic from the market.

While prescribing information to physicians had already called attention to the possibility of severe allergic reactions on this product, last month we began seeing an increasing number of reports of these reactions. After careful review, we decided that fullest protection of our users would be achieved by withdrawing ZOMAX while new labeling is being developed.

This decision, like those we made with TYLENOL, stems from our management philosophy. They are difficult and costly, but we haven't the slightest doubt that they are in the best long-term interests of our stockholders.

James E. Burke
Chairman;
Chief Executive Officer

New Brunswick,   David R. Clare
New Jersey   President;
March 17, 1983   Chairman of the Executive Committee

Johnson & Johnson
1988 Annual Report

Letter to Stockholders

1988 was another strong year of growth, with sales up 12.3 percent as we reached $9 billion in sales. Earnings per share rose 18.4%, yielding again this year an all-time high in return on stockholders' equity of 27.9% and a record net earnings margin of 10.8%.

The year was a particularly impressive one in terms of our ability to generate important new products in each of our three Sectors of business. ACUVUE disposable contact lenses were successfully launched in the U.S. by the Professional Sector, and are now being marketed internationally as well. The Pharmaceutical Sector introduced EPREX, the anti-anemia drug, into Europe, and we received approval from the Food and Drug Administration to market HISMANAL, the unique antihistamine, in the U.S. In the Consumer Sector, new SILHOUETTES Sanitary Napkins were introduced in Europe and TYLENOL Gelcaps continue to gain share of market following a highly successful introduction in the U.S.

Our research pipeline is demonstrating real vitality in all three Sectors, confirming our belief that our future success depends upon our ability to continue our aggressive investment in research and development. In 1988 we again increased our spending to $674 million or 7.5% of sales.

While all of us can take some pride in the current state of the business, we share a deep conviction that the underlying reasons for the successful performance of this Corporation are rooted in our philosophical beliefs.

As we have said before . . .

We believe the consistency of our overall performance as a Corporation is due to our unique and dynamic form of de-

centralized management, our adherence to the ethical princi-
ples embodied in our Credo, and our emphasis on managing
the business for the long term.

Our single most important role as Chairman and President has been to nurture and enhance these values over the past 12 years. Further, we are very confident that the Corporation's new leadership, composed of Ralph S. Larsen as Chairman and Chief Executive Officer, and Robert E. Campbell and Robert N. Wilson as Vice Chairmen of the Board of Directors, will ensure that these time-tested and highly pragmatic approaches to the business will continue . . . and that the results in the future will be every bit as impressive as they have been in the past.

At a time when this transfer of responsibility was taking place, it seemed appropriate to feature the management of our 171 companies in 54 countries as a reminder that it is their organizations that delivered the results of the past and that they bear a collective responsibility for the future. Our affiliate companies operate with considerable autonomy, and they share the same set of values and a common mission—improving health care everywhere in the world.

There is an extraordinary amount of interaction between and among our companies. Numerous examples of important synergy in research and development, marketing, operations and finance can be found within each of our Sectors, and increasingly across Sectors as well. The joint development by McNeil Consumer Products Company and Janssen Pharmaceutica of IMODIUM A-D in the United States is an excellent example. Janssen's IMODIUM is the leading antidiarrheal prescription product in the U.S. With the recent approval of the Food and Drug Administration, it is also being successfully marketed by McNeil Consumer Products Company as IMODIUM A-D, a liquid formulation that is more effective than any other non-prescription product on the market.

This kind of cooperation is one of the reasons we call ourselves the Johnson & Johnson Family of Companies.

As we make our last report to the stockholders, we are grateful for the opportunity to thank each and every person—some 81,000 in all—who make up this remarkable Family of Companies. We hope that you are aware of how important your individual endeavors are to our success, and that you will continue to gain personal satisfaction from the important work that you are doing.

We also want to thank you, our shareholders, for your loyal support, as well as our distinguished Board of Directors, who have been a constant source of strength to us in so many ways.

We want to take particular note of two of our Directors who will not be standing for re-election in 1989. Vic Dankis, after an outstanding career spanning over 35 years, has chosen to take early retirement. Dr. Irving London will not be standing for re-election as he has reached the mandatory retirement age. Dr. London joined our Board in 1982 and has been of great assistance to us all as a key scientific advisor. While they both will be missed on our Board of Directors, we are fortunate they will continue to contribute to the Corporation in a consulting capacity.

In February, 1989 the Board of Directors voted to recommend to the stockholders a two-for-one split of the Company's common stock. Quarterly dividends on the new shares will commence in June at 29 cents per share, an increase of 16%. These actions by the Board are a reaffirmation of the continuing strength of the business.

James E. Burke
Chairman;
Chief Executive Officer

New Brunswick,
New Jersey
March 15, 1989

David R. Clare
President;
Chairman of the Executive Committee

Johnson & Johnson
1990 Annual Report

Letter to Stockholders

Johnson & Johnson reached new highs in profitability in 1989, with net earnings exceeding $1 billion for the first time in our history. Earnings per share increased by 13.6%, yielding an all-time high return on stockholders' equity of 28.3%. Our net earnings margin was a record 11.1%. Despite lower currency exchange rates, our sales increased 8.4% to $9.76 billion. Excluding the effect of currency exchange rates, sales for 1989 would have increased 11%.

Product introductions in recent years helped fuel growth in 1989. HISMANAL Antihistamine and the ACUVUE Contact Lens were, for example, important factors in domestic sales growth. EPREX, used by dialysis patients suffering from anemia, and PREPULSID, a gastrointestinal prokinetic product recently introduced in Japan as well as other markets, both achieved strong sales gains internationally. More recently, we introduced in several major international markets the first diagnostic test for hepatitis C.

The growing demand for health care products such as these—sparked by better informed consumers and the trend toward positive lifestyles and prevention of disease—is spreading throughout the world. Fueled by the discovery of new medicines and technological advances, this demand is projected to continue well into the 21st Century. It assures the continued growth of the health care industry for as far as we can see into the future, and that means good things for Johnson & Johnson.

We enter the decade of the '90s with excellent financial strength and a sense of great optimism about our future. Our pharmaceutical product pipeline is the most extensive in the Company's history. Important new medical technologies are being developed and introduced in the Professional Sector. The consumer business has expanded its strategic presence with key acquisitions in Europe and a promising joint venture with Merck & Co. to develop and market over-the-counter drugs.

The challenge is to continue our substantial rate of growth in the face of vigorous, unrelenting competition. We start with the advantage of being a truly global corporation, with 175 companies selling products in most countries of the world and with numerous leadership brands in each of our business sectors. Our singleminded goal is leadership—in every market, in every business, and in every country in which we compete.

To meet the competitive challenge, we will continue to make substantial research and development investments and enhance our commitment to excellence in science and technology. We will strive to be the best-cost producer in every one of our businesses.

A measure of our investment in the future can be seen in both research and development and capital expenditures. Each exceeded $700 million last year, and for the past three years our total in these two areas was more than $3.5 billion. The research and development investment was in a broad range of products in the Consumer, Professional and Pharmaceutical Sectors.

The importance of this investment can be seen in such developments as PREPULSID, which treats digestive symptoms of chronic gastritis, and INTERCEED, the unique new product to prevent surgical adhesions. The successful interaction among our sectors is evident in the introduction of a consumer form of our prescription antidiarrheal, IMODIUM. The capital expenditures have mainly been to significantly improve our production facilities for existing products or to create production capability for new products, such as the ACUVUE lens.

These investments are very important but the fact is that the success of Johnson & Johnson begins with its people and ends with its people. We took several steps in the past year to let these outstanding people have the chance to work more productively, more efficiently and with greater personal satisfaction.

Part of that process is making sure that they are situated in organizations that make sense in today's intensely competitive marketplace. It had become evident to us that there was serious overlap in the functions and missions of several of our U.S. companies. Accordingly, we integrated three of our U.S. consumer products companies, combining the former Baby Products, Health Care and Dental Care consumer businesses into Johnson & Johnson Consumer Products, Inc. Similarly, we put the former Surgikos and Patient Care companies into a new professional company called Johnson & Johnson Medical Inc.

In the pharmaceutical area, we had earlier combined the research and development activities of four of our organizations into the R.W. Johnson Pharmaceutical Research Institute. Together with the Janssen Research Foundation Worldwide, this now gives us two first-class worldwide pharmaceutical research groups.

We have major initiatives underway to serve customers better. The Hospital Services organization has been more sharply focused. We also have made considerable progress in organizing innovative approaches to serve the retailers and distributors who sell our consumer products.

In the Consumer Sector, we took a significant initiative in our large worldwide market for sanitary protection products. We put in place a franchise management structure to coordinate the strategic activities of our many companies worldwide that sell these products.

We are seeing even greater levels of cooperation and interaction among our companies. For example, to enhance our efforts to discover and develop new skin care products, our Skin Care Council is composed of eight operating organizations engaged in skin care research.

Innovative technology and cost efficiency are the joint objectives of our efforts to bring our manufacturing processes and operations to a level that is unsurpassed in the world. Besides tapping outside academic, industrial and government resources, we have put renewed emphasis on creating unique manufacturing technology through our Office of Operations Technology and Development. We created the Johnson & Johnson Operations Institute. In cooperation with Duke University, we are sending managers there to benefit from the most advanced thinking in manufacturing and distribution technology.

Last year we made progress in implementing a new worldwide employee training strategy. This revitalization of employee training and development is a major investment in our employees to help them achieve their full potential. As an example, we have established an education and conference center in New Brunswick that will provide training for our people from all parts of the world.

We have now moved well along in the incorporation of the Quality Improvement Process throughout Johnson & Johnson. The objective is to give our people new skills and an understanding of the need to continually improve the quality of every aspect of our business.

All of these programs recognize that our human resources are the most important of all. We thank each of our dedicated employees around the world for their fine efforts.

We want to take this opportunity to thank two executives whose long careers with Johnson & Johnson have shaped the Company and the vision of many of the people who help run it today. James E. Burke and David R. Clare brought Johnson & Johnson to new heights of achievement during their stewardship. On behalf of the Board, we thank them for their many and unique contributions to the success of this business. They have been a wonderful example to us all.

As we enter this new decade, our objective is not only to meet the competitive challenge but to excel. On the following pages are current examples of some of the ways we are implementing our strategy to excel in the '90s.

Ralph S. Larsen
Chairman and Chief Executive Officer

Robert E. Campbell
Vice Chairman of the Board

New Brunswick,
New Jersey
March 14, 1990

Robert N. Wilson
Vice Chairman of the Board

EXCELLING IN THE '90s

Johnson & Johnson's goal is to be the best and most competitive health care products company in the world. To do so, we want to excel in several ways:

Leadership Brands

Our goal is leadership in every market, in every business, in every country in which we compete.

Better Value

Our objective is to be the best-cost producer in every business so we can produce meaningful products that contribute to well-being while providing good value for money spent.

Excellence in Science and Technology

We are committed to making substantial and increasingly productive investments in research and development.

Organizational Development

We want to create an environment that allows our people, our most important asset, to contribute to their maximum potential.

Johnson & Johnson
1997 Annual Report

Letter to Shareowners

1997 was another year of record sales and earnings for Johnson & Johnson. Revenue of $22.6 billion, an increase of 4.7% over 1996, represented the Company's 65th consecutive year of sales increases. Net income crossed the $3 billion mark for the first time to $3.3 billion, an increase of more than 14%. Basic earnings per share were $2.47, up 13.8%. This solid financial performance was achieved despite negative currency adjustments in many major markets throughout the world, intense competitive pressures in our principal businesses and virtually no net price increases.

Growth through innovation remains our single most important objective, at the sales line and—most importantly—in net income and earnings per share. That's how you build shareowner value.

Innovation, the theme of this annual report, is of extraordinary importance to the future of Johnson & Johnson. We are convinced that long term success in the new millennium will come only to those companies that value innovation and learn how to harness its power for growth. We have set our sights on leadership in health care on a global basis and we believe that innovation will propel us forward, to realize our long term vision.

Traditionally, innovation is most often thought of in the context of research & development and certainly that is important—we invested some $2.1 billion in research & development in 1997 and more than $8 billion over the past five years. That level of expenditure places us among the top ten companies in the United States. It has paid great dividends—giving us a steady stream of new products to fuel our growth. In fact, 36% of our 1997 sales came from new products introduced during the past five years, along with existing products launched into new markets during the same period. As critical as

Three Years in Brief Worldwide

(Dollars in Millions Except Per Share Figures)	1997	1996	1995	% Change 1997	% Change 1996
Sales to customers	$22,629	21,620	18,842	4.7	14.7
Net earnings	3,303	2,887	2,403	14.4	20.1
Cash dividends paid	1,137	974	827	16.7	17.8
Shareowners' equity	12,359	10,836	9,045	14.1	19.8
Percent return on average shareowners' equity	28.5	29.0	29.7	—	—
Per share*					
Net earnings—basic	$ 2.47	2.17	1.86	13.8	16.7
—diluted	2.41	2.12	1.82	13.7	16.5
Cash dividends paid	0.85	0.735	0.64	15.6	14.8
Shareowners' equity	9.19	8.13	6.98	13.0	16.5
Market price (year-end close)	64⅞	50½	42¾	28.5	18.1
Average shares outstanding (millions)—					
basic*	1,336.0	1,332.6	1,291.9	0.3	3.2
diluted*	1,369.9	1,359.4	1,317.4	0.8	3.2
Shareowners of record (thousands)	156.8	138.5	113.5	13.2	22.0
Number of employees (thousands)	90.5	89.3	82.3	1.3	8.5

*Adjusted to reflect the 1996 two-for-one stock split

research & development are . . . we take a much broader view of innovation. We believe that innovation must permeate every part of our organization—every functional area—and it must involve every one of our people throughout the world. That's where the real magic of innovation lies—and it is the key to our future.

Johnson & Johnson has become so large and broadly based in health care that it is sometimes difficult to fully appreciate the full range of promising growth opportunities we are pursuing and about which we are so excited. We call them "growth platforms" . . . and here are just a few of them:

Cardiology   Cardiology—and more broadly, the management of circulatory diseases—is an important growth platform. Through our Cordis affiliate, we are well positioned for a profitable future in cardiology and the treatment of circulatory diseases. While this business is intensely competitive, Cordis is moving forward with a substantial pipeline of new stent, balloon and endovascular products. We are particularly pleased with the merger of Biosense, Inc. into Cordis, for it brings new patented medical sensor technologies to facilitate a wide range of diagnostic and therapeutic procedures, particularly in the area of correcting heart rhythm problems.

Skin Care   Skin care is the largest consumer market in which we currently participate . . . some $47 billion at retail, and we believe we have the fastest growing skin care portfolio worldwide. Our presence extends from our wonderful heritage in baby products, to consumer toiletries, to prescription pharmaceuticals. Four of our five key skin care brands—NEUTROGENA, RoC, CLEAN & CLEAR and JOHNSON'S pH5.5—grew at double digit rates in 1997 and our baby skin care business strengthened its leadership position as well.

Wound Care   From BAND-AID Brand Adhesive Bandages, to genetically-engineered prescription products, to surgical sutures and staples, to unique tissue anchoring devices, we have a solid and profitable foundation for future growth. In 1997, we made significant progress in adding new technologies that are expected to accelerate our growth. Ethicon—the world leader in products for wound closure—licensed DERMABOND, which hopefully will receive marketing approval in 1998. It is a topical wound closure product that acts as a glue to quickly and painlessly close small wounds, reducing treatment time and trauma, while providing ease of use and lower overall costs. In addition, Ortho-McNeil received approval for REGRANEX Gel, a product of biotechnology research for the topical treatment of diabetic foot ulcers, which are so difficult to treat and heal.

Diabetes   LifeScan, a world leader in blood glucose monitoring, will shortly be introducing meterless SMARTSTRIP Test Strips in key markets outside the U.S. to allow people with diabetes to obtain accurate blood glucose values without a meter. LifeScan also has launched the SURESTEP PRO System for hospitals. Among other outside agreements, our interest in diabetes led to ongoing collaborations with other companies for the development and marketing of products for insulin-using patients.

Minimally Invasive Therapies   Ethicon Endo-Surgery continued to set the pace in minimally invasive therapies, with double digit growth in 1997. The company works with surgeons in developing new surgical procedures and in the design and development of related products. It also produces minimally invasive devices used in diagnostics.

Urology   The acquisition of Indigo Medical gave us entry and a solid platform for growth with minimally invasive technology in urology and related fields. The Indigo LASEROPTIC Treatment System, which received year-end marketing clearance for treating enlarged prostates in men—benign prostatic hyperplasia—combines fiber optics with diode laser technology. We also obtained worldwide marketing rights to TheraSeed Palladium-103, a radioactive isotope for treating localized prostate cancer.

Women's Health   The mergers in 1997 of Biopsys Medical into Ethicon Endo-Surgery and Gynecare into Ethicon, Inc., give us a much strengthened base in women's health care—particularly when added to Personal Products' line of sanitary protection products and Ortho-McNeil's expertise in vaginal antifungals, oral contraceptives and other family planning products. Biopsys produces products for minimally invasive breast biopsies and Gynecare markets minimally invasive devices for treating uterine disorders.

Vision Care   Vistakon has emerged as the market leader in the disposable contact lens business and makes more contact lenses than all of our competitors combined. This positions us to expand our opportunities across the vision care spectrum. We are planning to broaden beyond spherical contact lenses with the introduction of bifocal and other disposable contact lenses over the next two or three years. The acquisition of Innotech, Inc. in 1997 was an opportunity to further broaden our presence into the spectacle segment of the vision care market with interesting, innovative technology.

Pain Management Our nonprescription pain management product line, headed by TYLENOL Acetaminophen, was bolstered by the acquisition of adult MOTRIN Ibuprofen and we enhanced our growth potential in Japan by entering into a distribution agreement with Takeda. In the prescription category, DURAGESIC, a transdermal patch for chronic pain, and ULTRAM, a centrally acting analgesic, posted record sales. Our pipeline was strengthened through a licensing agreement for the rights to a novel class of compounds for treating pain and inflammation.

Nutraceuticals LACTAID lactose-intolerance products continue to post strong double digit sales in the nutraceuticals area. In 1997 we signed an agreement with Raisio of Finland for North American rights to the dietary ingredient stanol ester, sold as BENECOL. It has been shown to reduce cholesterol levels by 10–14%.

Central Nervous System We have been deeply involved with pharmaceutical products for the central nervous system for more than 30 years. Janssen-Cilag's RISPERDAL Antipsychotic achieved another year of very strong growth, and we are developing further indications for it. Ortho-McNeil's TOPAMAX, for the treatment of epilepsy, is a growing contributor and in the future we hope to bring to market new treatments for stroke and Alzheimer's disease.

Gastrointestinal From nonprescription acid control through our Merck joint venture and its category-leading brands PEPCID AC and MYLANTA, to IMODIUM, our market leader in anti-diarrheals, to motility agents such as PROPULSID and MOTILIUM, we have a rock-solid platform for future growth. We introduced nonprescription IMODIUM Advanced, for treating diarrhea plus bloating and cramps, and we added ACIPHEX (rabeprazole), a new proton pump inhibitor, to our gastroenterology pipeline via an agreement with Eisai. Internally, we are developing a promising prescription product for ulcerative colitis, and we are awaiting approval of MOTILIUM for diabetic gastropathy.

These selected growth platforms, and other important areas such as orthopaedics, hematology, oncology and hormone replacement therapy, are among the exciting opportunities that will energize the Company's long term growth. We will continue to strengthen our leadership positions in the broad categories in which we compete, and at the same time will seed, nourish and develop the many substantial growth platforms we are establishing for the future.

Progress in all of these therapeutic categories is helping us bring better health care to people around the world, and knowing that we are improving people's lives drives us in pursuit of our objective of growth through innovation. Towards this end, we will continue to employ four fundamental strategies:

1. *Internal Research & Development:* We intend to sustain our investment in research & development and are projecting spending in the range of $2.3 billion in 1998.

2. *In-Licensing and Outside Investments:* Over the past several years we have entered into 125–150 third party transactions annually, such as licensing arrangements, research collaborations and other alliances. Since 1990 our Development Corporation has invested over $300 million in more than 80 young companies, covering the full range of market opportunities from innovative technology in both our existing growth platforms as well as new ones.

3. *Acquisitions:* We will continue to aggressively pursue acquisition opportunities to build our business. Since 1990 we have made 34 acquisitions spanning a wide range of technologies and medical specialties. During the same time frame, we divested 15 businesses that no longer met our growth objectives.

4. *Productivity:* Thanks to the remarkable ingenuity of our people and our SIGNATURE OF QUALITY initiative, we are constantly improving all aspects of our operations and have taken about $2 billion in annual costs out of Johnson & Johnson since 1990. These efforts will be maintained as we work to provide good value to our customers and achieve superior financial performance, while at the same time making the necessary investments to build our business for the future.

Our balance sheet has never been stronger. We have no net debt and excellent free cash flow of more than $1 billion a year. We are one of only a handful of industrial companies still maintaining a Triple A credit rating. Our excellent financial condition provides us great flexibility to continue investing in the future of our business.

We also have a record of consistent dividend increases that few companies can match, and 1997 was the 35th consecutive year the dividend was increased, from $.735 in 1996 to $.85, up more than 15%. Our shareowners benefited further in 1997, as the total market value of Johnson & Johnson stock grew to $87.3 billion, an increase of nearly 30% over the prior year.

Johnson & Johnson's continued progress is testimony to the innovation, dedication and motivation of our extraordinary employees around the world, and we are deeply grateful for their contributions to our success. We wish to thank three of our directors, Philip Hawley, Thomas Murphy and Roger Smith, who are retiring after many years of dedicated service. We will miss their wise counsel and guidance. Fortunately, we have been able to attract two outstanding individuals to our Board, Henry B. Schacht, former chairman and chief executive officer of Lucent Technologies, and M. Judah Folkman, M.D., senior associate in surgery at Children's Hospital, Boston and professor, Harvard Medical School. Finally, and very importantly, we want to thank you, our shareowners, for your continued support and encouragement. We will continue to do our best to serve you well.

Ralph S. Larsen
Chairman of the Board and
Chief Executive Officer

Robert N. Wilson
Vice Chairman of the Board

March 11, 1998

What's new?

To reach beyond our imaginations and assure Johnson & Johnson's continued growth well into the 21st century, we have made a vigorous commitment to create an environment in which innovation flourishes throughout our companies around the world. We are nurturing a climate of innovative thinking among every one of our people, across all functions—not just in research and product development, in which we have a long and enviable track record. Hence the question: "What's new?" It is the way in which Dr. Paul Janssen, the founder of Janssen Pharmaceutica and one of our industry's great innovators, has often greeted employees over the years, in seeking new ideas as well as substantive feedback about progress towards achieving goals. We share the belief that long term success is embodied in an inquisitive culture in which people ask "What's new?" and focus on innovative ways of doing things, rather than conducting business as usual. The following pages provide some current examples of the innovativeness that is helping to assure a bright future for Johnson & Johnson.

Three Years in Brief Worldwide

(Dollars in Millions Except Per Share Figures)	2000	1999	1998	% Change 2000	% Change 1999
Sales to customers	$29,139	27,471	23,995	6.1	14.5
Net earnings*	4,800	4,167	3,003	15.2	38.8
Cash dividends paid	1,724	1,479	1,305	16.6	13.3
Shareowners' equity	18,808	16,213	14,077	16.0	15.2
Percent return on average shareowners' equity*	27.4	27.5	22.3	—	—
Per share					
Net earnings—basic*	$ 3.45	3.00	2.16	15.0	38.9
—diluted*	3.40	2.94	2.12	15.6	38.7
Cash dividends paid	1.24	1.09	0.97	13.8	12.4
Shareowners' equity	13.52	11.67	10.13	15.9	15.1
Market price (year-end close)	105.06	93.25	83.88	12.7	11.2
Average shares outstanding (millions)					
—basic	1,390.3	1,390.1	1,389.8	0.0	0.0
—diluted	1,417.4	1,418.2	1,417.2	(0.1)	0.1
Shareowners of record (thousands)	164.2	169.4	168.9	(3.1)	0.3
Number of employees (thousands)	98.5	97.8	94.3	0.7	3.7

*Net earnings and earnings per share for 2000, 1999 and 1998 include special charges of $33 million or $.02 diluted earnings per share for 2000, $42 million or $.03 diluted earnings per share for 1999 and $697 million or $.49 diluted earnings per share in 1998. These special charges relate to In-Process Research and Development charges and restructuring gains in 2000, the Centocor merger in 1999 and Restructuring and In-Process Research and Development charges in 1998. Excluding the impact of these charges, 2000 net earnings increased 14.8% over 1999. The percent return on average shareowners' equity in 2000 before these charges is 27.5%. For detailed discussion of these charges, refer to Note 14 and Note 17 of the Notes to Consolidated Financial Statements.

Johnson & Johnson
2000 Annual Report

Letter to Shareowners

The year 2000 was another very solid one for Johnson & Johnson. We continued to profitably build our business throughout the world with sales growing to $29.1 billion, an increase of 6.1% over 1999. On an operational basis, worldwide sales increased by 9.4% but were partially offset by the adverse effect (3.1%) of currency exchange rates. Net earnings for 2000 were a record $4.8 billion, an increase of 15.2% over the $4.2 billion we earned in the prior year. Earnings per share were $3.40, up 15.6% compared to $2.94 in 1999.

Over the past few years we have worked at increasing our cash flow from all of our businesses and in 2000 cash flow reached an all-time high of $6.6 billion . . . nearly double the $3.4 billion in cash flow generated just five years ago.

Among the many good things that result from a strong cash flow is the funding that is necessary to reinvest in building our business while, at the same time, increasing the dividends paid to shareowners. In 2000 we increased the dividend by 14.3%, from $.28 per quarter to $.32 per quarter—the Company's 38th consecutive year of dividend increases.

2000 was a year with a number of highlights, including the successful integration of Centocor into the Johnson & Johnson Family of Companies . . . the continued rapid growth of our pharmaceutical business . . . the resurgence of our important cardiology franchise, Cordis . . . and the successful completion of the restructuring of our worldwide manufacturing operations that was announced in late 1998.

2000 also was a year in which we once again learned that life is not an endless series of mountaintop-to-mountaintop experiences. As we became aware of potentially serious side-effects associated with our gastrointestinal medicine, PROPULSID, we decided in the interest of patient safety to restrict access to the product in many markets. While we were disappointed to have to take these measures with an important medicine that had benefited millions of patients over the years, in the final analysis we determined it was the right thing to do.

Our ability to achieve such strong business results in the face of the action we took on PROPULSID is a tribute to the resiliency of our people—their ability to adjust, redeploy spending, and move on in the face of adversity. Our people did a remarkable job of both meeting challenges and seizing opportunities during the past year, and we are deeply appreciative.

Research and development continued to be the foundation of our continued growth. In 2000 we invested $2.9 billion, an increase of 12.5% over the year earlier. Our commitment to scientific development has never been stronger and in 2001 we expect to invest about $3.3 billion in R&D.

Acquisitions remain an important part of our growth strategy, augmenting the new products and technologies flowing from our internal research and development. Over the past 20 years we have acquired 42 businesses, many of which have become important contributors to our growth. Companies such as Neutrogena, Cordis, DePuy, and Centocor are now important parts of the Johnson & Johnson family and have allowed us to establish leadership positions in important market segments.

To round out our growth strategy, we also operate our own in-house venture capital organization, the Johnson & Johnson Development Corporation, which has more than 100 investments in new and emerging companies and technologies.

Over the past 18 months, we've been particularly active in investing in the pharmaceuticals part of our business. In fact, during that time we've made 19 investments, many of which are at very early stages of development, including targets and new technologies that we believe have significant future potential.

While the Company actively seeks business-building mergers and acquisitions of companies and product lines, we also have in place a process to continually evaluate those businesses that are underperforming, or which no longer meet our growth objectives and would be better off in someone else's hands. Over the past 10 years, for example, we have divested 21 businesses or product lines.

The point is . . . we are engaged in an ongoing and disciplined process by which we seek out acquisition opportunities and work to ensure that our existing businesses achieve leadership levels of performance. These activities are a vital part of the process of renewal and rebirth that is essential to our sustained and profitable growth. They are among the ways in which we provide enduring shareowner value, as evidenced by our year-end market valuation of $146 billion—up from $25 billion 10 years ago.

Turning to the performance of our three business segments in 2000, the Pharmaceutical Segment continued its very strong growth. It is our largest and fastest growing segment. What was particularly remarkable about the performance of the Pharmaceutical business in 2000 is that the 15.2% growth in operational sales was achieved despite the severe decline in PROPULSID sales. The balance of the Pharmaceutical business grew by an exceptional 23.1%. Our Pharmaceutical business continues to be among the fastest growing in the industry.

It is noteworthy that our strong growth in pharmaceuticals comes not from a few, but from a wide range of products including PROCRIT/EPREX for treating anemia; RISPERDAL, an antipsychotic medication; LEVAQUIN, an anti-infective; DURAGESIC, a transdermal patch for chronic pain; REMICADE, a treatment for rheumatoid arthritis and Crohn's disease; ULTRAM, an analgesic for moderate to severe pain; TOPAMAX, an antiepileptic, and ACIPHEX/PARIET, a proton pump inhibitor for gastrointestinal disorders. Also notable is the fact that each of these products has substantial opportunity for further growth in their respective markets, and each has considerable patent life remaining.

At year-end 2000, Centocor received expanded marketing approval from the Food and Drug Administration for REMICADE, in combination with methotrexate, for inhibiting the progression of structural damage in patients with moderately to severely active rheumatoid arthritis who have had an inadequate response to methotrexate.

Centocor, together with Ortho Biotech, makes Johnson & Johnson the second-largest biotechnology company in the world, and we have considerable opportunity for continued rapid growth in this important field.

We launched REMINYL, for the treatment of mild to moderate Alzheimer's disease, in Denmark, the United Kingdom and Sweden. We also have approval of REMINYL in 14 other countries, and market launches are being planned. In the United States we have received an approvable letter for REMINYL from the FDA and are awaiting final approval.

The Professional Segment's 2000 operational growth of 6.9% was somewhat below historical levels, having been impacted substantially by a number of divestitures. Adjusting for the net effect of acquisitions and divestitures, the Professional group had solid growth of 8.4% from internal operations.

DePuy added to its major position in orthopaedic joint reconstruction and, through its AcroMed organization, is developing a strong position in products for repair of the spine. One of the top two orthopaedic companies in the world, DePuy is the market leader in knee implants and has a strong number two position in the rapidly growing spine market.

Among the leadership positions we have built in the Professional Segment are Ethicon in wound closure; Ethicon Endo-Surgery in products for minimally invasive surgery, and Vistakon in contact lenses.

During the past year we strengthened each of these leadership positions but we made our most dramatic progress in the field of cardiology with Cordis, which has gained significant market share in Europe and the United States, with the Bx VELOCITY Coronary Artery Stent.

We expect to see Cordis make further gains with the introduction of its newly approved heparin-coated stent, for helping to maintain normal arterial blood flow. Cordis also is well along in the development of a "pharma stent" that is coated with the drug Sirolimus, for preventing arterial scarring or restenosis. This is, potentially, a very important development for patients worldwide. Among other recent accomplishments, Cordis received FDA approval of the CHECKMATE System for gamma radiation of in-stent restenosis, and its acquisition of Atrionix brings us a company with promising technology for treating atrial fibrillation—a condition for which there is no truly effective treatment currently available.

Diagnostics business highlights included Ortho-Clinical Diagnostics' continued strengthening of its performance and cash flow and LifeScan's introduction of the new ONE TOUCH Ultra Meter for measuring blood glucose levels—featuring alternate body site testing, a very small, one microliter sample size, and a rapid five-second test time.

The Consumer Segment remains a steady performer with operational growth in the 4% range. Many of our consumer brands carry the JOHNSON & JOHNSON name and over the years they have made it more than a trademark . . . it has become a "trustmark" known in virtually every country of the world.

We have been focusing intensely on building our skin care business, which now includes such well-known, successful brands as NEUTROGENA, RoC, JOHNSON'S pH5.5, CLEAN & CLEAR, and AVEENO. Strength in the worldwide skin care franchise has been helping to drive Consumer Segment sales, to go along with our other important leadership positions such as nonprescription pharmaceuticals.

As we look to the future, our objective is to achieve superior levels of profitable growth . . . to capitalize on opportunities to build our business to the benefit of customers, patients, the medical community and you, our shareowners.

To move the Company forward to new heights, we entered the current decade with the organization focused on four fundamental imperatives that we believe are essential to our continued growth: Innovation . . . Process Excellence . . . The Internet . . . and Flawless Execution.

And so the theme of this Annual Report is "Imperatives for Growth." We have challenged the men and women of Johnson & Johnson throughout the world to assume the responsibility of implementing these imperatives. Accordingly, we thought it would be appropriate to feature some people from our management ranks and examples of ways in which they are fulfilling this mandate.

Innovation: The innovation imperative . . . and its encouragement to pioneer . . . cuts across the entire Johnson & Johnson organization and is vitally important to our future. We encourage our people to question everything we do to make us more innovative. We want an organization made up of inquisitive people, for we are seeking innovation—constant improvements in the ways people do their jobs—in all areas of the business. Conducting "business as usual" does not belong in an inquisitive culture.

For a Company engaged in health care, it is of vital importance that we quicken the pace of research and development. Our 9,000 focused R&D personnel are working hard at finding new and better ways to conduct their research, using the latest tools available.

Process Excellence: The second management imperative is Process Excellence. It is an extension of THE SIGNATURE OF QUALITY initiative, which for the past several years has been an important part of our worldwide drive for continuous improvement. Process Excellence consolidates all of our learning into a proven and high-powered methodology that incorporates such concepts as Six Sigma, Design Excellence, and quick, robust, Lean Thinking.

While our Company is highly decentralized and we pride ourselves on giving our managements a great deal of running room, Process Excellence is not optional. It is a process that we have made mandatory throughout our entire Company. It is nothing less than the application of martial arts training and discipline. It starts with rigorous training in statistical analysis and problem solving techniques, and it includes developing metrics and dashboard measurements for virtually any process in the organization.

SOQ Process Excellence is not simply a cost reduction effort, although it surely does reduce costs. The implementation of Process Excellence has been an important contributor to the productivity efforts that have helped us to take almost $5 billion in costs out of the Company over the past five years. To put it another way, that means our annual operating costs today are $5 billion lower . . . and we believe we have just scratched the surface.

Perhaps the biggest payoff from Process Excellence is that it helps to drive growth. It reduces the time required to develop new products and it gives us greater confidence in the efficacy of our new products. We are convinced that Process Excellence makes us a more formidable competitor at every level, and it drives both volume and profits.

The Internet: Our objective under the third imperative, the Internet . . . is to become the best-connected health care company in the world. We anticipate that the Internet will enable us to change the ways we conduct business within and among our 194 companies, helping us to capture economies of scale while maintaining our decentralized management structure.

We are pursuing strategies around three principles:

- Using the Internet to create new ways of connecting with our customers, including physicians, hospitals, consumers and retail partners.

- Transforming our core business processes—redesigning the ways we work—in order to take full advantage of the Internet technology to save time, money, and improve quality.

- Creating a Web-savvy culture throughout our entire employee base around the world, recognizing that the Internet is an important tool in everything we do—at work and at home.

More than 1,000 of our senior leaders have been through Internet immersion forums. At Johnson & Johnson, if you're not skilled in the use of the Internet, you're probably an endangered species.

Flawless Execution: The idea is to instill in every one of our businesses around the world the clear understanding that in order to continue to drive the Corporation's profitable growth, we are dependent upon the "flawless execution" of each business unit's plans, and we rely upon them to deliver on their financial forecasts. This requirement is crucial because of the breadth and diversity of our health care businesses, as well as our decentralization.

With our well-known aversion to bureaucracy we simply have to have confidence in our operating units to develop their own business plans against their own target markets . . . and then deliver on their promises. This is especially important if we are to continue to meet both short term and long term performance targets.

These four management imperatives—Innovation, Process Excellence, The Internet, and Flawless Execution—form the basis for heightened growth and improvement of an organization that already is performing exceptionally well.

Guided by the ethical principles embodied in Our Credo, which helps create a common bond among the people in our far-flung affiliates, we continue to manage Johnson & Johnson for the long term. Our fundamental mission is to pursue the growth of this enterprise based on providing scientifically sound, high quality products and services that help heal, cure disease, and improve the quality of life for people everywhere. That is our mission and we take it seriously.

The strength of our executive leadership is fundamental to Johnson & Johnson's continued growth and success in the years ahead. Early in 2001, we made a number of important management changes that will increase the depth of our leadership talent. James T. Lenehan and William C. Weldon were elected Vice Chairmen of the Board of Directors and members of an expanded Office of the Chairman. Additionally, Michael J. Dormer and Robert G. Savage were named as members of the Executive Committee. These exceptional executives have acquired many years of diverse experience in a wide range of our businesses. All have demonstrated their commitment to our Credo values and are business-builders with proven track records. We are fortunate to have them in these key leadership positions.

This is a wonderful time in health care. New advances in medical knowledge are leading to new diagnostic and treatment modalities of all kinds. The exploration of the mysteries of the genome are bringing new discoveries each day. This in turn is leading to ever-increasing worldwide demand for new and innovative medicines and technology-based products that diagnose, treat and cure disease—and do so more cost effectively than ever before. All of us at Johnson & Johnson consider it a great privilege to be a part of it.

Johnson & Johnson now has nearly one hundred thousand people around the world. They are good and decent people . . . the best you will ever meet . . . and they are working very hard to make important contributions to the betterment of humankind and to the success of our business. We thank them for their efforts and dedication. And we thank you, our shareowners, for your continued encouragement and support.

Ralph S. Larsen
Chairman of the Board and
Chief Executive Officer

Robert N. Wilson
Senior Vice Chairman of the Board

March 14, 2001

Imperatives for Growth

To ensure sustained growth and build enduring shareowner value over the long term, Johnson & Johnson has set its sights on four broad priorities or imperatives for the decade ahead: Innovation, Process Excellence, The Internet, and Flawless Execution. The pages that follow provide examples of some of the ways in which individuals from the ranks of our decentralized management are leading the implementation of these imperatives throughout the world.

● *Innovation*

The key to growth lies in innovation. We have a passionate focus on innovation and we are nurturing an environment in which an innovative culture flourishes throughout our 194 companies. Our goal is to create a climate of continuous, relentless innovative thinking among every one of our people, across all functions.

● *Process Excellence*

THE SIGNATURE OF QUALITY (SOQ) Process Excellence initiative encompasses proven and high-powered improvement methodologies that incorporate Six Sigma, Design Excellence and quick, robust Lean Thinking approaches. Process Excellence has been an important contributor to productivity efforts that have helped us to eliminate more than $5 billion in costs over the past five years. We now have more than 1,800 experts trained in problem solving and making fundamental improvements—800 at the "Black Belt" achievement level and over 1,000 "Green Belts."

● *The Internet*

The Internet is an essential part of our strategy for growth and our goal is to be the best-connected health care company in the world, as recognized by our customers. We anticipate that the Internet will enable us to change the way we do business, capturing economies of scale within our decentralized management structure. We are connecting with customers in new and better ways . . . Web-enabling key business processes to improve speed, quality and costs . . . and we are strengthening links to hospitals, physicians and patients.

● *Flawless Execution*

The day-to-day execution of our strategies and business plans is crucial to our success and it is the responsibility of the men and women who make up our decentralized management teams. Throughout the world, we strive to meet competitive challenges by implementing business-building initiatives with speed, excellence and precision . . . with flawless execution.

Glossary of Investing Terms

advance

An increase in price of a stock; opposite of *decline*.

advance/decline line

The ratio of the number of stocks that rose divided by the number of stocks that fell during a certain period. Measures the general direction of the stock market: if greater than 1, a *bull market;* if less than one, a *bear market.*

aggressive

An investment strategy in which the investor risks losses to pursue above-average returns.

American Association of Individual Investors (AAII)

A non-profit organization that provides education and advice for individual investors.

American Stock Exchange (AMEX)

After the New York Stock Exchange (NYSE), the second-largest exchange in the United States.

AMEX Market Value Index

An index that tracks the performance of over 800 companies listed on the AMEX.

annual meeting

A meeting held by a public company at the end of the fiscal year, in which the company's shareholders elect directors for the company.

annual report

A report required by the Securities and Exchange Commission (SEC) for public companies to send to shareholders at the end of each fiscal year. Includes the company's financial status for the year and a projection of future activities. Contains the balance sheet, income statement, and a glossy brochure detailing the company's finances.

annual return

The percentage of increased value of an investment over a one-year period.

appreciation

The measure of an asset's increase in value; opposite of *depreciation*.

ask

The lowest price that a prospective seller is willing to take for a particular security or commodity.

asset

Any item possessing economic value owned by an individual or corporation. Includes securities, accounts receivable, inventory, property, etc.

asset allocation

The manner in which an investor or company chooses to divide investments among different types of assets, depending upon the individual's or company's financial situation as well as risk and reward goals.

asset classes

Different categories of assets, including stocks, bonds, mutual funds, real estate, and cash.

asset/equity ratio

A company's total assets divided by shareholder's equity.

authorized stock

The maximum number of shares of stock a company can issue, as determined by the company's initial charter and modified by shareholder vote.

average

The unweighted arithmetic mean of a group of stocks that represents the overall market or a specific subset of it. Example: The Dow Jones Industrial Average (DJIA).

balanced investment strategy

An investment portfolio management strategy that provides increased income while avoiding undue risk.

balance sheet

A financial statement that provides a snapshot of a company's financial condition at a certain time period. Lists assets, liabilities, and net worth.

Banking Act of 1933

A Depression-era act of Congress meant to aid the country's financial situation and increase stability by separating commercial banking from investment banking.

barometer

Certain economic and market data used to gauge overall financial trends, including interest rates, consumer spending, unemployment rates, and housing starts.

base period

A certain time period used as a benchmark to measure financial trends.

basis

The original price paid for an investment at the time of purchase.

bear market

A market in which stock prices are falling, generally to 20% below their highest trading prices. Pessimistic investors who expect the market to decline are known as "bears."

Beige Book

A report on current market conditions, published eight times a year by the Federal Reserve Board.

bellwether

A certain stock whose performance is believed to indicate overall market trends.

beta

The quantitative measure of a stock's risk relative to the overall market. Stocks with a number greater than one are considered riskier than the overall market, while those with a beta below one less volatile than the average.

bid

> The highest price a prospective buyer is willing to pay for a security at a given time. Opposite of *ask*.

Blue Chip

> The stock of a large, well-established company with a solid record of earnings and dividend payments over a long period.

Board of Directors

> A body of individuals elected by a company's shareholders and entrusted with the management of the company.

book value

> A company's net worth, or common stock equity, as it appears on a balance statement. Book value is equal to assets minus liabilities, as well as intangible assets such as goodwill. Book value per share is book value divided by common shares outstanding.

broker

> An individual or firm that acts as an intermediary between buyers and sellers of securities.

bubble

> A market condition when the economy is overvalued, and stocks have risen so far that they are going to crash or "burst."

bull market

> A period during which stock prices are rising consistently, usually by 20% or more. "Bulls" or "bullish" investors are those who believe a certain stock or the overall market is about to rise.

business cycle

> A long-term pattern of market activity, with alternating periods of economic growth and decline.

buy

> The exchange of money for ownership in a security or other asset. Also, an order indicating that an investor wants to purchase a security.

buy and hold

> A long-term investment strategy to buy and hold shares over several years to minimize capital gains taxes on profits.

buyer's market

A market with low prices and more sellers than buyers, created by an excess of supply over demand.

capital gain

The amount by which an asset's selling price exceeds its initial purchase price, or basis. Opposite of a *capital loss*.

capitalization

The market price of all common stock, preferred stock, and bonds issued by a company.

capital structure

The mix of long-term debt and equity maintained by a company, including outstanding common and preferred stock, as well as retained earnings.

cash flow

A measure of company finances, equaling cash receipts minus cash payments over a certain period of time.

certificate

A physical document that indicates ownership of a stock or bond.

certificate of deposit (CD)

A savings instrument offered by a bank with a fixed interest rate based upon a set term. CDs offer a low risk and low return investment.

Chief Executive Officer (CEO)

An executive responsible for overseeing a company's operations. Often the CEO is also the chairman of the company's Board of Directors.

Chief Financial Officer (CFO)

An executive responsible for a company's financial planning and record-keeping.

Chief Operating Officer (COO)

An executive in charge of day-to-day management of a company.

civilian unemployment rate

A percentage based on the total number of unemployed people divided by the number of total workers, both employed and unemployed.

class action suit

A specific type of lawsuit brought by one representative party on behalf of a group of individuals all similarly situated or affected by an illegal activity.

close

A final market price, or closing price, for a security at the end of a trading session.

coattail investing

A risky investment strategy whereby an investor tries to duplicate the performance of another successful investor as soon as their trades are made public.

coincident indicator

An economic indicator directly related to, and which varies with, a certain economic trend.

commission

A fee charged by a broker or agent for facilitating a purchase or sale transaction for an investor.

Commodities Futures Price Index

An index of futures prices, including livestock, energy, agriculture, and metals. Trends in this index indicate inflationary activities.

commodity

An interchangeable, physical raw material, such as food, grain or gold. These products are traded on a *commodities exchange* (COMEX).

common stock

Securities representing ownership in a corporation. Common stock shares generally come with voting rights, but in the event of dividend distribution or liquidation, common stockholders' rights to the company's assets are secondary to those who own bonds and preferred stocks.

composite

An average or index which combines multiple averages. For example, the Dow Jones Composite index combines the industrial, transportation, and utility averages.

Compound Annual Growth Rate (CAGR)

The growth rate of a company's investment on average, per year, over a multiple-year period.

confidence indicator

A measure of consumer faith in the economy and stock market, considered an indicator of overall economic health.

conservative

A cautious investment strategy that seeks to minimize risk and preserve capital.

Consumer Price Index (CPI)

A measure of the monthly change in price in a fixed group of consumer products and services, including food, housing, and transportation. Published by the Labor Department.

Cost of Living Adjustment (COLA)

An annual change in wages to adjust to fluctuations in the consumer price index.

countercyclical

A trend that moves in the opposite direction of that of the overall economic cycle.

crash

A large and sudden drop in market prices or downturn in economic conditions.

current assets

On a balance sheet, the group of assets that can be converted to cash, sold, or consumed during the next 12-month business cycle.

current liabilities

On a balance sheet, the sum of financial obligations that will become due during the next 12-month business cycle, including taxes, wages, and debt.

current ratio

Current assets divided by current liabilities.

cycle

One complete movement of economic or market conditions.

cyclical industry

An industry with performance closely tied to overall economic conditions.

day trade

A buy and sell of securities on the same day.

debt

An obligation to pay back money borrowed by a specified date, with interest. Includes bonds, loan notes, and mortgages.

debt/equity ratio

The value of a company's long-term debt divided by common shareholders' equity.

deflation

A general decline in price levels for consumer goods and services. The opposite of *inflation*.

demand

Consumer desire and ability to purchase goods and services.

depreciation

The loss in value of an asset over time, measured for tax and accounting purposes.

depression

An economic period of downturn characterized by declining business activity, falling prices, and decreased consumer demand.

dilution

A reduction in a company's earnings per share that would result from the conversion of convertible securities to common stock.

dip

A small, temporary drop in stock price.

diversification

An investment strategy designed to minimize risk by allocating money over a variety of types of investments, including stocks, bonds, and real estate.

divest

To sell off all or part of an investment.

dividend

Regular payments made by a company to its shareholders in the form of cash or stock.

Dogs of the Dow

Portfolio strategy that includes buying the ten Dow Jones Industrial Average stocks with the highest yield.

dot-com

A company with an Internet-based business model.

Dow Jones Averages

The leading measure of overall stock market conditions, includes three weighted averages published by Dow Jones & Co. (listed below).

Dow Jones Industrial Average (DJIA)

The price-weighted average of 30 "blue chip" stocks of the largest U.S. industrial companies.

Dow Jones Transportation Average

The price-weighted average of 20 of the largest U.S. transportation companies.

Dow Jones Utility Average

The price-weighted average of 15 of the largest U.S. utility companies.

downturn

A decline in overall economic health or market conditions.

dual listing

The listing of a company's stock on more than one market exchange.

earnings

The total revenues from a company's operations, minus their operating expenses and taxes.

earnings per share (EPS)

A company's total earnings, or losses, divided by the number of common shares outstanding. Calculated annually and quarterly.

economic indicator

Key statistical indicators of the nation's overall economic direction, such as unemployment rate, inflation, and consumer confidence.

Employer Cost Index (ECI)

Published by the Department of Labor on a quarterly basis, the measure of changes in employee wages and benefits over a variety of industries.

Equally Weighted Average

An index that gives equal weight to each stock, regardless of price.

equilibrium price

A market price for an item at which the supply equals demand.

equity

Ownership interest in a corporation, usually in the form of stock.

ethical investing

A portfolio strategy that focuses on investing in companies with ethical business activities.

Federal Reserve Board

A governing body that oversees twelve regional Federal Reserve Banks, sets monetary policies, and monitors the country's overall economic health. Also called "the Fed."

fiduciary

An individual or organization that holds assets and has the authority to make financial decisions for another party.

financial statement

A regularly published written report that quantifies a company's financial situation. Includes an income statement and current balance sheet.

fiscal year

A year-long financial accounting period that does not necessarily begin and end on January 1.

fixed asset

A long-term, tangible asset used in business operations, such as property or equipment, not expected to be converted to cash in the next fiscal year.

Forbes 500

Annual ranking of the top 500 public companies in the United States, published by *Forbes* magazine.

forecast

A prediction of future economic trends based upon current activities.

Fortune 500

Annual listing of the 500 largest industrial corporations in the U.S., published by *Fortune* magazine.

gain

An increase in stock price or asset value.

General Agreement on Tariffs and Trade (GATT)

United Nations-affiliated treaty organization that facilitates international trade.

Generally Accepted Accounting Principles (GAAP)

Widely-used national standards for financial information reporting, as established by the Financial Accounting Standards Board (FASB).

globalization

Increasingly global investment strategy and business environment.

going public

When a company begins offering its shares to the public, in an initial public offering.

goodwill

Valuable intangible assets in business, such as reputation and brand recognition.

Gross Domestic Product (GDP)

The total market value of all goods and services produced in the United States in a year.

Gross National Product (GNP)

The Gross Domestic Product, plus all domestic income as a result of investments abroad.

hard landing

A sudden economic change from an expansion period to a recession.

hi-lo index

An average of the number of stocks that reach new price highs and lows each day, as a measure of overall market health.

historical data

Information about a company's past activities and performance, used to predict the company's future.

housing market index

An economic index that measures the demand for new homes.

housing starts

A measure of the number of single and multi-family residential units for which construction has started within a specified time period.

illiquid

Assets, such as real estate, that cannot be quickly converted into cash.

Implicit Price Deflator

A gauge of overall inflation activity, based upon price changes and fluctuations in the GNP.

income statement

A company's financial statement that summarizes profits and losses, revenues and expenses over a period of time.

index

A measure of a group of stocks, either weighted or unweighted, used as a benchmark to gauge overall financial or economic performance.

indicator

Set of statistical data that provides information about certain markets or the overall economy, including inflation, employment, and interest rates.

individual investor

An individual who buys and sells small amounts of securities, as opposed to an *institutional investor*. Also called a *retail investor*.

inflation

A general increase in the cost of consumer goods and services. Opposite of *deflation*.

initial public offering (IPO)

A company's first offering of stock to the public.

institutional investor

As opposed to an individual investor, a large investing entity such as a bank or fund.

intangible asset

A company's valuable non-physical asset such as good will, intellectual property, or brand recognition.

intellectual property

An intangible asset consisting of knowledge and ideas, such as a patent, trademark, or copyright.

investment club

A group of individual investors who pool income for joint investments.

investment company

A company that charges fees to make joint investments on behalf of individual or retail investors.

investment income

Income derived from a portfolio of investments.

investment strategy

A guiding plan for investment activities. Allocation of assets among various types of investments, including stocks, bonds, cash, and real estate.

laggard

An underperforming investment.

lagging indicator

An economic indicator that becomes apparent *after* the overall economy has changed, including labor costs and unemployment rate.

large cap

A company with a total market capitalization of over $5 billion.

leaders

Stocks that have performed the best over a specified time period.

leading indicator

An economic indicator that changes before the overall economy has changed, including money supply and building permits. Published monthly by the Commerce Department to predict future economic activity.

limit order

A customer's request to buy or sell a security only at a specified price, usually placed while waiting for the price to move in a volatile market.

liquid asset

An asset that can readily be converted to cash.

liquidate

To convert assets to cash by selling all or some of a company's assets.

liquid market

A market with a high number of buyers and sellers.

listed

A stock traded on a major securities exchange, such as the NYSE or the AMEX.

listing requirements

Set of conditions companies must meet in order to be listed on a particular stock exchange, including minimum market capitalization or income, or number of outstanding shares.

loss

The reduction in value of a stock or other asset.

market

The stock market, or the place where buyers and sellers transact securities exchanges.

market order

A customer's request to buy or sell as quickly as possible at the best price currently available.

market price

The last reported price at which a security has been bought or sold.

market-share weighted index

A stock index or average in which each stock affects the index in proportion to its number of outstanding market shares.

market value

The total dollar value of a security based upon its number of outstanding shares and their market price.

market-value weighted index

A stock index or average in which each stock affects the index in proportion to its market value.

mid cap

A company with a total market capitalization of $1 billion to $5 billion.

monopoly

The situation that exists when one company dominates the market for a particular good or service.

mutual fund

A group of diversified security investments managed by an investment company on behalf of individual investors.

National Association of Investors Corporation (NAIC)

A non-profit educational organization designed to teach individual investors or investment clubs how to invest in stocks.

National Association of Securities Dealers (NASD)

A self-regulated industry organization that operates the NASDAQ stock market.

National Association of Securities Dealers Automated Quotations System (NASDAQ)

An NASD-owned computerized system designed to track price quotations and facilitate trades of over-the-counter stocks.

National Market System

The trading system for over-the-counter stocks as supervised by the NASD and NASDAQ.

net

The amount remaining after certain deductions have been made.

net change

The difference between the closing price of a security on one trading day and that of the previous day. Referred to as the bid price for over-the-counter stocks.

net income

A company's total earnings based upon revenues minus expenses (including depreciation, interest, and taxes). Same as *net profit*.

net worth

A company's or individual's total assets minus total liabilities.

new issue

A security being offered for sale to the public for the first time. Also called an initial public offering (IPO), these issues must comply with specific SEC regulations.

New York Stock Exchange (NYSE)

The United States' oldest and largest stock exchange.

Nikkei Index

An index that tracks the 225 leading stocks on the Tokyo Stock Exchange.

noncurrent asset

An asset that is not readily convertible to cash within the next year. Includes *fixed assets* and *intangible assets*.

note

A written, short-term debt security, which usually matures within five years.

NYSE Composite Index

An index that tracks the market value fluctuations of all common stocks traded on the NYSE. The NYSE also provides indexes on four sectors: industrials, utilities, transportation, and finance.

odd lot

A group of less than 100 shares of stock to be bought or sold.

order

A client's request to a securities broker to buy or sell a certain amount of stock at a specific price or at the market price.

over-the-counter (OTC)

A security that is not listed on a major exchange, and the trading of which is monitored by the NASD. Usually the stock of small cap companies, trading at $1 or less.

panic

Sudden fear of market collapse, leading to falling stock prices. Generally precedes or accompanies a market "crash."

par

A nominal sum, or "face value" assigned to a security when issued by the company, generally bearing no relationship to its market price. Par is the amount repaid to the purchaser of a bond when it matures.

passive management

An investment strategy that seeks to mirror the composition of an index or market segment in order to stay even with the overall market.

Pink Sheets

A daily listing of market prices for over-the-counter stocks not included on the daily NASDAQ listings.

point

A measure of a security's price increase or decrease. For stocks, generally $1 per share.

portfolio

A collection of assets or investments owned by an individual or company.

preferred stock

A company's capital stock that confers on its owners precedence over common stockholders in the event of dividend payments or company liquidation.

price/earnings ratio (P/E ratio)

The ratio of a stock's capitalization divided by its after-tax earnings over a year-long period (or the price of the stock by the earnings per share). Generally used to measure how expensive a stock is, as compared to companies in the same market sector.

price range

A stock's lowest and highest prices during a certain period, usually a year.

price to book ratio

The ratio of a stock's capitalization divided by its book value, either on an entire company or per-share basis.

price to sales ratio

The ratio of a stock's capitalization divided by its sales for the previous 12 months, used to compare against the performance of other companies in the same market sector.

price-weighted index

A stock index or average in which each stock affects the index in proportion to its price per share.

prime rate

The interest rate that commercial banks charge large corporations. Considered a lagging economic indicator.

private company

A company that does not trade shares of its stock on the open market.

Producer Price Index (PPI)

A measure of the monthly change in wholesale price levels in the economy published by the Bureau of Labor Statistics. This index is an inflationary indicator.

profit

The measure of gain from an investment after subtraction of expenses.

profit margin

A company's percentage of net profit after taxes divided by sales for a year-long period.

public company

A company whose stock is issued through offerings and traded on the open market.

qualitative analysis

A valuation of an investment based on non-numeric factors, such as brand reputation, employee morale, and management capabilities.

quantitative analysis

A valuation of an investment based upon numeric factors, including market share, revenues, and earnings.

quarterly

A 3-month-long fiscal period, used for reporting earnings.

quarterly report

A form required by the SEC for all public companies to report financial results by quarter. Also called *Form 10-Q*.

quick ratio

The measure of a company's current assets divided by current liabilities, used to evaluate a company's liquidity.

recession

A period of economic decline and reduced activity, for two or more consecutive quarters.

record date

The date by which an individual must own shares of a company to be entitled to a dividend.

recovery

Following a recession in the business cycle, a period of increased economic activity and rising GDP.

regional exchange

A smaller stock exchange that generally lists corporations in its geographic region.

relative strength

A stock's price movement over a period of time relative to the movement of a market index, such as the S&P 500.

research and development (R&D)

Experimentation and acquiring knowledge about products and services in order to make improvements and fill market needs.

Retail Price Index (RPI)

A measure of the change in price in a fixed group of retail goods. This index is an inflationary indicator.

retained earnings

Earnings that a company does not pay out as dividends to shareholders, but uses to pay off debt or re-invest in the business.

return

The annual return on an investment as a percentage of the total amount invested.

Return on Assets (ROA)

A measure of a company's fiscal year earnings divided by total assets, indicating the company's profitability.

Return on Equity (ROE)

A measure of a company's fiscal year after-tax income divided by book value, indicating the company's success in re-investing earnings.

Return on Investment (ROI)

The measure of the percentage of profit made on an investment, equal to the fiscal year income divided by stock equity plus long-term debt.

reverse split

A decrease in a company's number of outstanding shares and a proportionate increase in the price per share, usually done to disguise falling stock prices and maintain market capitalization.

risk-averse (investing)

Following a conservative investment strategy.

round lot

A normal trading unit of 100 shares of stock or multiples of 100.

Securities and Exchange Commission (SEC)

The federal agency responsible for regulating the securities industry and protecting investors against fraudulent practices.

security

An investment instrument that represents ownership in or obligation to a business or government entity.

selloff

A sudden decline in stock prices resulting from widespread selling.

share

A certificate representing ownership in a corporation.

shareholder

An individual who owns shares of common or preferred stock in a corporation.

split-adjusted price

The price per share of a stock after a stock split. For comparison between past and current stock prices, historical prices are adjusted to reflect subsequent splits.

Standard & Poor's 500 (S&P 500)

A market-value weighted index of 500 blue chip stocks, emphasizing industrial companies but also including industrial and transportation corporations. Considered a reflection of the stock market as a whole.

standards

Products, services, or technologies that become so pervasive as to dominate a market.

stock

A share of ownership in a corporation.

stock exchange

A marketplace in which shares of stock are bought and sold, including the NYSE and AMEX.

stock index

An index of the market prices of a particular group of stocks, such as the S&P 500.

stock market

General term for the buying and selling of stocks through exchanges and over-the-counter.

stock split

An increase in a company's number of outstanding shares of stock and a proportionate decrease in the price per share, which maintains a security's market capitalization. Usually done to drop the stock price per share to make investment more accessible to small investors.

supply

The total amount of a good or service available for sale; varies along with demand to determine price.

tangible asset

An asset having a physical existence, such as real estate or cash. Opposite of *intangible assets* such as goodwill and reputation.

tear sheet

A nickname for S&P stock reports, which provide financial information on public companies.

tick

The smallest fluctuation in a security's price, either upward or downward (1/8 for stock and 1/32 for bonds).

ticker symbol

A combination of letters used to identify a stock. Stocks listed on an exchange have ticker symbols consisting of three letters, and those on the NASDAQ have four or five letters.

topping out

A stock or market that has had a period of rising prices and is now expected to stay steady or decline.

total return

The percentage profit on an investment over a given time period, including dividend and interest income.

total return index

An index that measures the performance of a group of stocks by assuming that all dividends and distributions are reinvested. Includes the S&P 500 and the Wilshire 5000.

trade

A transaction in which one party buys a security or commodity from another party.

trend

A general direction of economic movement.

undercapitalization

When a business lacks sufficient money to perform normal business activities.

underperformer

An investment with a smaller return than that of similar investments.

undervalued

When a security is priced below its perceived value based on price/earnings ratios.

upside

Potential for gain or profitability.

uptrend

Upward price movement of the overall market or a particular stock.

valuation

Processes for determining the value of a particular stock, asset, or company.

value averaging

An investment strategy whereby an investor buys more shares of stock when market prices drop and fewer when prices rise. Also called *dollar cost averaging*.

Value Line

An index of approximately 1,700 NYSE, AMEX, and NASDAQ stocks tracked by the Value Line investment survey.

Value Line Investment Survey

A publication offering condensed, single-page financial reports for investors regarding widely held stocks.

volatility

The measure of fluctuations in a stock's price over time.

volume

The number of shares traded for a certain stock or a whole exchange over a specified period of time.

Wall Street ("the Street")

Name of the financial district in lower Manhattan in New York City, where the NYSE and AMEX are located. Also refers to the investment community in general.

weighting

The relative influence of certain stocks when combined into an index, as based on various features such as price, outstanding shares, or market value.

Wilshire 5000 Equity Index

A market-value weighted index including all AMEX and NYSE stocks, as well as more active over-the-counter stocks.

working capital

The measure of a company's current assets minus its current liabilities.

yield

The percentage annual rate of return on an investment. Equals annual dividends divided by the purchase price.

Index